ALTERNATIVE DISPUTE RESOLUTION LAWS

MADHUMITA PAUL

Contents

Preface

The settlement of the disputes beyond the four walls of the courts of law is what the future holds for us. Litigation is time consuming, complex and expensive justice dispoensation system. ADR is a neutral array of hyrbrid procedures that seeks to provide accessible justice at low cost.

This book comes as a handy reference to the students purely made with exam-oriented approach having covered wide range of topics to give the students a broad idea of the subject. This book will help the students to understand each and every topic minutely and score good marks in the examination.

Acknowledgements

I am really grateful to my parents, to my professors in my law college and to everyone who has been an inspiration for me throughout this project to sucessfully execute it. Wthout the support, efforts, contribution and sacrifice of each one of you, it would have been impossible for me to write this book. I am loss at words to thank everyone.

My sincere thanks are to Notion Press Publication House for publishing this book with utmost care and co-operation.

CHAPTER ONE

INTRODUCTION TO ALTERNATIVE DISPUTE RESOLUTION

1. Write a brief note about ADR.

Answer

Alternative Dispute Resolution (ADR) is a term used to illustrate diverse one of a kind modes of resolving legal disputes. It is experienced each through the enterprise global & not unusual men because it is almost impracticable for all individuals to document regulation fits and get justice on time. The Courts are backlogged with schedules resulting in putting off for a year or more for the applicants to have their cases heard and decided. To resolve this trouble of backlogged instances and not on time choices ADR Mechanism has been evolved in reaction. ADR techniques are being increasingly more established in subject of regulation and commercial sectors both at National and International levels. The numerous techniques of ADR can assist the parties to resolve their issues at their very own terms cheaply and rapidly. In growing countries in which almost, every person opts for litigation to clear up their disputes, there may be excessive burdening of instances on courts, which has in the end led to unhappiness among people regarding the existing state of affairs of judicial system and its ability to dispense justice. This opinion is based totally at the famous perception of, "Justice delayed is justice denied". However, the blame for the backlogged instances in those developing countries can not be attributed to the Courts & inflexible judicial gadget on my own. The important purpose behind the delayed justice is the non-implementation of negotiation methods earlier than litigation. It is against this flaw that the mechanisms of alternative dispute decision are being brought in these countries which may be very vital for the easy functioning of the judicial machine. These ADR mechanisms, that have been operating efficiently in presenting a cordial and speedy answer for problems in evolved economies, are being certainly amended as a result and applied with a view to strengthen the judicial machine of the developing countries. The term "Alternative Disputes Resolution" includes numerous modes of agreement that are, Lok Adalats, Arbitration, Conciliation and Mediation. This approach of ADR has been utilized by many evolved nations for effective disputes decision. The maximum usually practiced amongst other types of Alternative Disputes Resolution is Mediation. Mediation as a tool for alternate dispute decision isn't a brand new idea. To put it in easier terms, mediation is a non violent settlement of disputes with the engagement of an unbiased third-party who acts as a facilitator and is referred to as a 'Mediator". The different techniques of ADR can help the parties to settle their disputes at their personal phrases & situations cheaply and expeditiously. ADR techniques are further to the Courts in character. These strategies can be beneficial in almost all contentious matters, which can be able to being settled, legally, by using agreement between the parties. ADR strategies may be engaged in several classes of disputes, especially civil, business, business and family disputes. From the look at of the specific ADR techniques it is determined that, alternative dispute decision techniques offer brief solution with respect to industrial disputes where the monetary growth of the Country rests. Alternative Dispute Resolutions is an alternative way to the formal & rigid court system. It is an alternative to avoid litigation. It is because of the fact that the Courts are overburdened with tens of millions of instances. ADR best gives a replacement choice to litigation. It is meant simplest to complement and now not supersede the criminal device. It may be engaged in civil, commercial, commercial and family disputes. It could be very vital in all kinds of industrial disputes and is taken into consideration to offer the quickest solution in admire of enterprise disputes of worldwide person. Even if the ADR proceeding fails, it's far in no way a waste of money and time worried since it enables the parties to see every others function at the case and apprehend the case higher. It is essential to distinguish among which shape of Alternative Dispute Resolution is binding and which are non-binding. Among all of the available techniques, negotiation, mediation and conciliation are non-binding paperwork, and rely upon the consent of both the parties to reach a mutual agreement. Binding ADR strategies produce a 3rd-party selection that each the parties ought to follow even though they disagree with the end result similar to a judicial choice. Non-binding Arbitration produces a third-party celebration choice that the parties might also reject and may even appeal inside the court of regulation.

2. Explain the various techniques of ADR.

Answer

The phrase "Alternative Dispute Resolution" includes numerous negotiation mechanisms including, Lok Adalats, Arbitration, Conciliation, and Mediation in its fold. Several countries have used this Alternative Dispute Resolution strategy for successful dispute resolution. Mediation is the maximum commonplace form of alternative dispute resolution. In addition to this, a few had defined mediation as the maximum suitable approach for resolving disputes. Mediation as a device for resolving disputes isn't a new idea. To positioned it absolutely, mediation is a friendly dispute settlement involving a impartial 0.33 party celebration who serves as a facilitator and is referred to as a' mediator. ADR is typically much less formal, much less high-priced and less time consuming than traditional trials. ADR also can give human beings a more possibility to decide while and the way to settle their warfare. Arbitration, Conciliation, Mediation, Judicial Settlement, and Lok Adalat are the most normally used ADR techniques in civil complaints. Section 89 of the Code of Civil system allows for the out-of-courtroom resolution of disputes. It is based at the Law Commission of India's and the Malimath Committee's recommendations. The Law Commission of India cautioned that the Court can also inspire any party to a healthy or action to wait in individual for you to locate an amicable resolution of the disagreement. The Malimath Committee advocated that it be made compulsory for the Court to refer the battle to arbitration thru Arbitration, Conciliation, Mediation, Judicial Arbitration via Lok Adalat, after the issues have been framed. The case ought to only continue similarly if the parties refuse to solve their variations through any of the alternative dispute decision strategies.

The special methods of ADR can be summarized as under: –

Arbitration: Arbitration, a kind of alternative dispute decision (ADR), is a method for resolving conflicts outside of the courtroom machine in which the parties to a confrontation refer it to one or more human beings, referred to as arbitrators, to whom they intend to be certain with the aid of their judgment. It is a way of dispute agreement in which a third person examines the proof inside the case and renders a legally enforceable choice for both parties. Arbitration awards have restricted proper of review and appeal. Arbitration isn't always similar to civil and mediation court cases. Arbitration can be optional, or obligatory. Clearly, mandatory arbitration can most effective come from a law or arrangement that is together signed in which the parties conform to arbitrate all contemporary or future disputes without necessarily understanding what disputes will ever arise. In India, if the problem is mentioned Arbitration then the provisions of the Arbitration and Conciliation Act, 1996 will apply. The main types of arbitration are (a) Voluntary Arbitration; (b) Compulsory Arbitration, (c) Ad-hoc Arbitration; (d) Institutional Arbitration; (e) Statutory Arbitration; (f) Domestic or International Arbitration.

Conciliation: It is a form of alternative dispute resolution wherein the parties to a dispute hire a conciliator to assist them remedy their troubles individually. They try this by using decreasing conflicts, strengthening coordination, figuring out issues, supplying technical help, discussing viable solutions and bringing about a negotiated settlement. In this manner, it is a chunk distinct from Arbitration. It is a consensual method wherein the parties worried are free to reach a settlement and try to solve their war of words through conciliation. The approach is flexible, which enables the parties to decide the time, duration and content material of the conciliation procedure. Those court cases are seldom public. These are interest-based totally, because the conciliator need to remember not only the legal positions of the parties but additionally their; economic, economic and/or personal hobbies when negotiating a agreement. In the Indian experience, the phrases conciliation and mediation are synonymous. Conciliation is a cooperative mechanism through which the conciliator, a certified and expert impartial, enables negotiations among the disputing parties and assists them in recognizing their variations and desires to be able to attain an association this is mutually suitable. Once a agreement has been found earlier than a conciliator between the parties to the conflict, the decision has the impact of an arbitration award and is legally tenable in any court. Many exchange disputes, in which it isn't important that a binding and enforceable choice should take location, are subject to conciliation. Conciliation may be specifically suitable wherein the parties to the battle searching for to hold and maintain their commercial members of the family.

Mediation: Today, mediation is a voluntary and informal approach of dispute decision for the disputing parties. It is an easy, voluntary, celebration-focused and dependent negotiation process wherein an impartial third party facilitates parties clear up their disputes friendly using distinctive communiqué and negotiation techniques. Mediation is a manner wherein the parties are themselves on top of things of it. The mediator's function is exactly that of a facilitator, assisting the parties in achieving a negotiated agreement in their disagreement. The mediator takes no selections and does not implement his opinion on what have to be a truthful settlement. Both facets meet with a skilled impartial mediator at some point of the mediation procedure. The session starts with each aspect explaining the issue from their factor of view, and the treatment they are looking for. Once the respective perspectives of each party celebration is mentioned, the mediator then splits them into non-public rooms, starting up a "caucus convention" technique and then "joint meetings with the parties." Both facets conform to the restrict. The mediator does not have the power to dictate his decision concerning the party. Mediation permits a war to be treated rapidly, with minimum pressure and price, while still preserving the parties' courting and retaining anonymity.

Judicial Settlement: Section 89 of the Code of Civil Procedure refers to judicial settlement as one of the alternative modes of resolution of disputes. The term "Judicial Settlement" is however specified in Section 89 of the Code. It was provided that the provisions of the Legal Services Authority Act, 1987, would apply when there is a judicial settlement. This means that the Judge concerned, seeks to settle the dispute between the parties in a legal settlement amicably. Such settlement shall be deemed to be an agreement within the scope of the Legal Services Authority Act, 1987, if any friendly settlement is resorted to and reached in the case at question.Section 21 of the Legal Services Authorities Act, 1987 specifies that each Lok Adalat award shall be deemed a Civil Court decree. India has no written guidance on judicial settlement.

Lok Adalat: The idea this is gaining recognition is that of Lok Adalats or the courts of the people as shaped by way of the government to settle disputes through conciliation and compromise. It is a judicial frame and a dispute agreement organization installed for social justice with the aid of the citizens themselves, primarily based on the agreement or agreement acquired through formal negotiations. The first Lok Adalats turned into carried out as far back as 1982 in Una village of Junagadh (Gujrat). Adalats also recognize instances inside their jurisdiction which are pending in regular courts. Section 89 of the Code of Civil Procedure additionally gives for the attraction to the Lok Adalat of pending civil disputes. When the matter is cited the Lok Adalat then it'll comply with the provisions of the Legal Services Authorities Act, 1987. The maintaining of Lok Adalat is governed through Section 19 of the Legal Services Authorities Act, 1987.

3. What are the advantages and disadvantages of ADR techniques? Mention.

Answer

<u>**ADVANTAGES**</u>

The advantages of ADR techniques are:

ADR is beneficial for resolving any important dispute. The result varies from situation to situation but effects are more effective than that of legal process. There are few key benefits of ADR:

(a) Cost Saving: One of the biggest reasons parties choose to remedy their disputes outside of the courts is fee. Judicial method for resolving any disputes involves court fees, documentation costs, recommends costs and plenty of different extra charges. Moreover, if there's corruption present, the price may also rise even higher. ADR does no longer contain professional expenses or courts expenses. Alternative dispute decision commonly expenses plenty less than litigation, permitting smaller monetary disputes a financially feasible manner to be settled. ADR also saves the cash of presidency.

(b) Speed: Adjudicative process for resolving conflicts are very prolonged when you consider that there are courtroom selections upon which the hearing is dependent. Litigation can take over a year to remedy because of exceptional timing and dates concerned. Matters that are being solved using the ADR approach may take months or maybe just weeks to be resolved. ADR may be organized by way of the parties and the panelist as quickly as they're able to meet. Compared to the court docket procedure, wherein waits of 2-3 years are regular, dispute resolution is as fast as the parties want it to be.

(c) Control: The parties have control over some of the approaches in ADR. Usually choosing the technique of ADR, selecting the panelist for the dispute decision; the period of the method; and, in a mediations case, even the outcome are controlled and maintained with the aid of the parties. In case of lawsuit manner, the manipulate is absolutely possessed with the aid of the court and superb authority. Opposed to the court device, in which the criminal device and the decision to manage each aspect; ADR is a lot extra bendy. Furthermore, inside the case of arbitration the parties have some distance more flexibility in selecting the software of applicable enterprise standards, domestic law, the law of a foreign United States of America, a unique set of rules used by the arbitration service, or maybe non secular regulation, in some cases.

(d) Confidentiality: Privacy is completely securitized in terms of Alternative Dispute Resolution. ADR is carried out in non-public, therefore keeping off exposure from the media. The public also are not able to attend. On the alternative hand disputes resolved in court are public and the judgments offered are also in public. ADR affords sure decision procedures inclusive of, Mediation, arbitration, and mini trials which might be conducted in private maintain strict confidentiality.

(e) Experienced Neutral Panelists: The panelists are professional mediators and arbitrators with schooling and information in dispute resolution. Disputing parties are capable of selecting ther panelist from a list of qualified folks that are specialized in specific area of dispute. In the courtroom gadget, binding choices are made with the aid of judges who may also lack expertise in one-of-a-kind practices.

(f) Cooperative Approach: All ADR services take place in a extra informal, much less confrontational environment. This is extra conducive to keep a high quality enterprise dating between the 2 parties. With mediation, mainly, the result is collaboration between the 2 parties. Therefore ADR is a procedure that appears into the first-point of settlement procedure of each party which will finish a compromised mutual choice.

(g) Flexibility: Legal and non-felony disputes can be addressed all through this technique proving it to be bendier. Some may think that is a suitable package in the sense that it takes into account fundamental issues of the parties and gives treatments no longer available when at court.

(h) Parties into Good Terms: The intention of ADR is to discover a compromise answer which is pleasant to both parties. Court lawsuits create a winner and a loser. Using ADR to settle a dispute way companies can remain on true terms and preserve to alternate with each different as soon as their dispute is resolved.

DISADVANTAGES

There are numerous disadvantages blocking off the way of a success dispute resolution and often affecting both parties sentiment to accept a compromised decision. Some the risks are:

(a) Unequal Bargaining Power: In positive conditions one facet is capable of control the alternative. Therefore a vast imbalance of electricity exists. For example: employment and divorce cases, making the courts a better choice for a weak party.

(b) Lack of Legal Proficiency: Where a dispute entails difficult legal points a mediator or arbitrator is unlikely to have the equal criminal know-how and information as a decision. Dispute can be of various situations including, industrial conflicts, social conflicts, prison conflicts and many others which require specialized mediator. In most of the cases the mediator does no longer possess a decisive factor of view.

(c) No System of Specific Model: It isn't clean to expect the outcome of a dispute decided through ADR as there is no machine of precedent. Therefore, it is far less difficult to acquire proof from the other celebration in a lawsuit. Lack of system consequences in restrained prediction of results.

(d) Enforceability: Most types of ADR aren't legally binding, making any award tough to put into effect. Legal arbitration has a few sort of manner for internal appeals, which permits the choice as binding and simplest concern to the evaluation of courtroom.

(e) Required Court Action: The arbitrator's selection can require a courtroom order if one of the parties refuse to simply accept the arbitrator's selection. This could now not best create chaos however additionally an obligatory assessment through the court docket. Thus, ADR on occasion raises the query of biasness of arbitrator's selection. Also, there's very restricted opportunity for judicial evaluation of an arbitrator's choice. A court may overturn an arbitrator's choice if it decided problems that had been now not inside the scope of the arbitration settlement.

(f) Might no longer be a Good Fit: Alternative dispute resolutions typically resolve simplest issues of money or civil disputes. Alternative dispute resolution lawsuits will no longer result in injunctive orders. They can't result in an order requiring one of the parties to do or give up doing a specific affirmative act.

(g) Limits Discovery Process: ADR commonly intending without the protections supplied parties in litigation, together with the ones rules governed through discovery. Courts commonly permit a awesome deal of latitude inside the discovery system, which isn't energetic in opportunity dispute resolution.

CHAPTER TWO

COMPARATIVE STUDY OF PRINCIPAL TECHNIQUES OF ADR

1. What are the differences between arbitration and litigation?
Answer
The differences between arbitration and litigation are as follows:

a. Arbitration process is private between the two parties whereas litigation is conducted in a courtroom.
b. Arbitration is an informal method of dispute resolution whereas litigation is a formal procedure of resolving the disputes.
c. Arbitration process is quick whereas court room process is lengthy.
d. Arbitration starts as soon as the arbitrator is appointed whereas in litigation, a case must wait until it arrives the court to hear.
e. The cost of the process of litigation is limited to the fee of the arbitrator and attorney fees whereas litigation involves court costs which are fairly high.
f. The parties in the arbitration appoint the arbitrator whereas in litigation there is no scope for the parties to appoint the deciding authority.

2. Point out the differences between arbitration and negotiation.
Answer
The differences are as follows:

a. The neutral 3rd party appointed to decide the dispute in arbitration is called the arbitrator whereas the same person in negotiation is called the facilitator or the negotiator.

b. In arbitration, an arbitrator is appointed by both parties while a facilitator oversees a negotiation.

c. The decision in arbitration is called arbitral award whereas the decision given by the facilitator in negotiation is called memorandum of agreement.

d. The decision of the arbitral award is legally binding whereas the settlement arrived at negotiation is not legally binding as an award.

e. Arbitrators are usually lawyers or people associated with the law while facilitators may not have a law background.

f. An award (in arbitration) cannot be appealed to a court. On the other hand, a court can question or overturn a memorandum of agreement that transpired as a result of negotiation.

3. Explain the differences between arbitration and mediation.

Answer

The differences are as follows:

a) A technique of conflict settlement wherein a neutral 3rd party, assist the parties concerned in arriving at decision, agreeable to all, is referred to as mediation. Arbitration is a private trial, wherein a rational 3rd party examines the dispute, hears the parties involved, gathers information and pass on choice.

b) Mediation is collaborative, i.e. wherein the parties work collectively to arrive at a selection while arbitration is adverse in nature.

c) The process of mediation is a bit casual even as arbitration is a proper procedure, that's similar to a courtroom room hearing.

d) In mediation, the third party performs the position of facilitator, in an effort to facilitate negotiation. On the opposite, the arbitrator plays the position of a judge to render a choice.

e) There can only be one mediator, in the mediation. As in opposition to this, more than one arbitrators or panel of arbitrators may be there in arbitration.

f) In mediation, together with the joint conferences, the mediators hear both the parties inside the personal meeting. On the flip aspect, in arbitration, the arbitrator remains impartial, and no such non-public communiqué takes place. Thus the judgment is based on evidentiary hearings.

4. What are the differences between arbitration and conciliation?

Answer

The differences are as follows:

a) Arbitration refers to a technique of resolving industrial disputes, in which the management and the labor present their respective positions to the impartial third party, who takes a decision and imposes it. Conciliation is a way of resolving the dispute, in which an independent person, who meet parties jointly and severally and enables them to reach at negotiated settlement or remedy their differences.

b) The choice made by using the arbitrator is suitable to the parties concerned. On the opposite hand, the conciliator does no longer have the right to implement his choice.

c) Arbitration requires a previous agreement between parties called arbitration agreement, which needs to be in writing. As against this, the process of conciliation doesn't require any pre-agreement.

d) Arbitration is to be had for the current and future disputes whereas the conciliation can be adopted for current disputes most effective.

e) Arbitration is like a court proceeding, in which witnesses, evidence, cross-exam, transcripts and legal suggest are used. Conciliation is a casual manner of resolving disputes among the management and labor.

5. What are the differences between mediation and conciliation?

Answer

The differences are as follows:

1. In mediation, the facilitator should be unbiased and objective to the gatherings' debate, while with negotiation the facilitator assumes a more dynamic part.

2. In mediation, the gatherings are urged to track down an answer, with the facilitator just going about as an aide. While with negotiation the facilitator has the obligation to distinguish the targets of the gatherings and effectively assist with tracking down an answer.

3. In mediation, the facilitator doesn't give any judgment. With negotiation, the facilitator additionally assumes the part of evaluator and intervener that base the arrangement on what is considered the most useful arrangement as per the facilitator.

4. It isn't important to observe a goal with regards to mediation, yet the point is an understanding. With negotiation, a goal is a vital result and is executable as a declaration of the common court.

5. Mediation is represented by the Code of Civil Procedure Act, 1908. Negotiation is represented by the Arbitration and Conciliation Act, 1996.

6. Confidentiality has a significant influence in the two cycles; be that as it may, they are authorized in an unexpected way. In mediation privacy depends on trust, and is it encouraged for all gatherings to sign a Confidentiality Clause for additional action. Confidentially in not set in stone by the law.

7. Mediation mediates when a significant struggle or debate have emerged that needs proficient mediation. Negotiation is utilized preventively and means to stop a debate to forming into something real.

6. Point out the differences between mediation and negotiation.

Answer

The point of differences between mediation and negotiation are:

1. Negotiation is a strategy to determine modern questions through self-advising and conversation between the party individuals or the delegates of the gatherings, wherein a commonly adequate understanding is looked for. Actually, mediation is a non-legal proportion of debate settlement, where a neutral third party is welcomed, to work with conversation, and recommend elective negotiations, to bring understanding.

2. While negotiation doesn't include the mediation of an neutral third party, in an mediation cycle, the middle person is welcomed or assent is given by both the gatherings to examine the issue with the arbiter, to achieve an appropriate elective negotiation.

3. When it comes to gatherings, representatives of the gatherings to struggle meet to advance their inclinations, requests and talk about their freedoms. As against, in mediation, the middle person meets the gatherings to struggle both together and independently, to talk about the place of issue and propose negotiations.

4. Negotiation is a strategy to determine modern questions through self-advising and conversation between the party individuals or the delegates of the gatherings, wherein a commonly adequate understanding is looked for. Actually, mediation is a non-legal proportion of debate settlement, where a neutral third party is welcomed, to work with conversation, and recommend elective negotiations, to bring understanding.

5. While mediation doesn't include the mediation of an unbiased outsider, in a mediation cycle, the middle person is welcomed or assent is given by both the gatherings to examine the issue with the arbiter, to achieve an appropriate elective negotiation.

6. When it comes to gatherings, delegates of the gatherings to struggle meet to advance their inclinations, requests and talk about their privileges.

As against, in mediation, the middle person meets the gatherings to struggle both mutually and independently, to examine the mark of issue and propose negotiations

CHAPTER THREE

MEDIATION, NEGOTIATION AND CONCILIATION

1. Write an exhaustive note on Mediation as an effective tool of ADR mechanism.

Answer

An Alternative Dispute Resolution is a result of all such issues which are looking by the public continually in the prosecution. It resembles a substitute to the conventional strategy for settling debate and equity. An ADR component principally centers around conveying equity through shared assent of the gatherings in the base time immediately like in case. An ADR instrument perceived four techniques to determine any debate like intervention, appeasement, mediation and arrangement. Elective strategies are work on the common agreement and attempt to resolve question with as soon as practicable. ADR system is a choice to the public who would rather not go for regular strategy or need to determine their matter without courts impedance. These systems enjoy their own benefit as well as defects, similar to some other interaction have might do. However, especially with regards to intervention, it needs accentuation that this is just one of the significant targets. Mediation as a processual mediation in the overall set of laws satisfies other instrumental and natural capacities which are of an equivalent, in the event that not more noteworthy significance. In its instrumental capacity, intervention is a way to satisfying expressed destinations. The inherent capacity of intervention underlines the worth of mediation as an end in itself. It is a non-restricting technique wherein an unprejudiced outsider, the conciliator or arbiter, helps the gatherings to a question in arriving at a commonly acceptable and concurred settlement of the debate. Mediation is a process by which questioning gatherings connect with the help of a nonpartisan outsider to go about as an arbiter. In India, the law and practice of private and conditional business questions without court mediation can be traced all the way back to antiquated times. Assertion or intervention as a choice to debate goal by civil courts has been predominant in India from Vedic times. The earliest realized composition is the Bhradarnayaka Upanishad, where different sorts of arbitral bodies viz the Puga, the Sreni and the Kula. These arbitral bodies, known as Panchayats, managed assortment of questions, for example, debates of authoritative, wedding and even of a criminal sort. The disputants would usually acknowledge the choice of the panchayat and henceforth a settlement showed up resulting to pacification by the panchayat would be however restricting as the choice that might have been on clear lawful commitments.

Each course of ADR instrument has its own fundamental standards on which it's work and giving positive results. Like as other process mediation has its own key standards which are useful in resolving debates between the gatherings on their shared agreement. Parties pick intervention process over case might be a result of these standards which have given powerful way to the interaction. Intervention typically has found in the family matters or any adjoining issues which could be resolve by mediation process instead of going to court for equity.

a) Parties ought to take an interest intentionally: It is fundamental that nobody ought to compelled to intervene, it ought to be in the possession of gatherings and they need to conclude whether they need to intercede or go to the courts. Parties have their intentional interest in the intervention interaction. it will be more productive. Individuals will collaborate all the more completely on the off chance that they realize they are allowed to leave anytime. This draws in their own freedom of thought and feeling of direction and empowers them to drive the process towards arrangement rather than to be directed to a comprehension by an outsider. Assuming they drive the process they are more dedicated to the result.

b) Confidentiality matters all the while: Within the actual mediation the go between should not uncover any confidences that are imparted to them except if allowed to do as such. Except if somebody shares a criminal purpose or act that includes damage to self or other. In regard of additional procedures (besides with the express authorization of the two sides). For individuals to have a good sense of security to investigate their apprehensions and nerves the interaction should be seen to be altogether secret. All the data given in the mediation will be kept classified and it can't be utilized in the court procedures neither by the go betweens nor court can inquire as to why the intervention didn't work.

c) Mediators are fair: The go between should act fair-mindedly and impartially. He/she ought to see all standards of mediation and think about just matters of technique. He/she ought not remark, esteem decisions, nor offer guidance or recommending arrangements. Unbiasedness of a go between ought to guarantee that the gatherings acknowledge him/her as a genuinely committed individual to settling the question and who favors the two sides in the debate, looking for arrangements that would fulfill the two sides in the debate. The go between should remember that his/her conduct, disposition, and now and then the procedures of intervention can bring a feeling of compassion towards one side. Whenever that occurs, then, at that point, the intervention went the incorrect way. The go between can't fill the role assuming there are conditions that show questions about his unbiasedness and objectivity.

d) An arrangement must be settled with the fulfillment of gatherings concerned: The obligation regarding characterizing the issue, setting the plan and concurring the arrangement rests with individuals in the debate. The intervention method can be begun provided that there is an arrangement between the gatherings. Intervention won't be begun without the two players proposing to determine the question. In such cases, intervention is abused uniquely as a mean of keeping the court interaction and keeping what is happening at "the state of affairs". A third party has to know how to clarify the benefits of such question goal to the gatherings, with the goal that they, when all is said and done, deliberately consent to be essential for such interaction. The gatherings ought to be educated on the likelihood to interfere with the mediation interaction at any stage, on the off chance that they express requirement for such. The guideline of ability applies at all phases of the procedures. A party or the arbiter may whenever pull out and afterward move the case to the appointed authority. A go between can interfere with mediation if he/she feels that gatherings get some distance from the arrangement or that are significantly more gone against than they were toward the beginning of intervention. The fundamental guideline during the time spent mediation is that the intervention technique ought not hurt the gatherings at all, however to add to the goal of their debate. Considering that mediation is just an enhancement to the court procedures, it should not keep a party from practicing the right of admittance to court and utilization of legal insurance.

e) Mediation is without bias to different techniques: It is critical that individuals maintain whatever authority is needed to summon different measures. Assuming the mediation were viewed as an upheld strategy or one that eliminates a singular's rights it would contract the imagination and expands the potential for opposition.

The utilization of the expression "mediation" is notable in International Law. It is the specialized term in International Law which implies the mediation by an unbiased and cordial state between two States at war or just before battle with one another, of its great workplaces to reestablish or to safeguard harmony. The term is at times as an equivalent word for mediation, yet intervention contrasts from it in being absolutely a cordial demonstration. Mediation at one degree of insight is a method for staying away from the entanglements of case. The issues which emerge in the goal of debates through case are notable. These are, comprehensively: delay, cost, unbending nature of methodology and a decrease in the participatory job of gatherings. In the way of settling these traps of suit, mediation is the most often taken on ADR methodology. The course of mediation might need to go through a few phases, for example, opening proclamation, opening explanation to the gatherings, summing up and plan setting, investigation of issues, private meetings or assemblies, joint exchange meeting, understanding. A third party might take on either a facilitative or evaluative methodology. Middle people attempt to stay away from assessments and decisions. They rather work with and urge gatherings to open up their interchanges and unveil their inclinations and needs. In this interaction the arbiter gets the chance of finding the marks of contrast and the area of discussion or question. He may then assist the gatherings with overcoming any barrier between them.

The substance of mediation lies in the job of the go between as a facilitator. The third party isn't an adjudicator. Dissimilar to the Judge in a customary Court setting or besides even a referee, the go between is neither an adjudicator of realities nor an authority of questions. The job of the third party is to establish a climate wherein parties before him are worked with towards settling the debate in a simply deliberate settlement or understanding. The go between is an impartial. The lack of bias of the third party is likened to the nonpartisanship of a Judge yet the job of the go between is totally not the same as that of a Judge. The go between doesn't either convey judgment or direct to the gatherings the provisions of the understanding.

Mediation is a compelling ADR component should be visible to these 4 advantages of the interaction, for example,

a) Informality: No court rules or legitimate points of reference are associated with intervention. The arbiter doesn't force a choice upon the gatherings. Instead of ill-disposed gatherings, the go between assists with keeping an efficient way to deal with settling a question. There are no decent arrangements in mediation. Gatherings can hope to creating savvy fixes to determine matters and the arrangement rests with the actual gatherings.

b) Privacy and classification: The mediation meeting happens in a private setting, for example, a gathering room at any of the Arbitration Associations. Intervention doesn't involve openly available report. Its secrecy is kept up with.

c) Time and cost reserve funds: Mediation by and large keeps going a day. Complex matters might require additional time because of profoundly specialized issue or potentially different gatherings. Without the conventions found in suit, mediation as a rule brings about significant costs reserve funds.

d) Control: Parties have command over their support in mediation. A party can choose to end their support anytime in mediation. Go betweens assist parties with keeping up with command over the exchange that takes place.

There is no vital obstruction of court in ADR methods yet in various stages court would have release a few significant capacities. The intervention isn't mediation of cases however in the resolving debate. Go between is additionally not permitted to arbitrate yet can attempt to resolve debate or could speak with the gatherings.

Execution of the interaction doesn't intend to take each case under mediation yet at first it ought to apply on the little plot of cases and in the wake of seeing the achievement execution should be possible on huge number of cases. Mediation is a critical process for lessening trouble from the legal executive and it is adequately skilled to shifts the concentration from mediation towards settling or resolving debate under principal overall set of laws.

It is more facilitative for the advancement of regulation to move toward preventive process not at all like suit arranged methodologies as it were. Most importantly, trust in the mediation interaction will be cultivated provided that the go between releases in certain terms the moral worries of a process to which the job of the third party is central.

2. Write a brief note about negotiation.

Answer

Negotiation is a procedure of examining issues among one selves and coming to a resolution helping all engaged with the conversation. It is quite possibly the best method for keeping away from clashes and strains. At the point when people disagree with one another, they sit together, talk about issues on an open discussion, haggle with one another and come to an elective which fulfills all. In a layman's language it is likewise named as haggling. Negotiation is fundamental in corporates as well as private lives to guarantee harmony and bliss. Exchange is better as it would forestall ruining your connection with your bosses later.

Moderator: An individual addressing an association or a position who pays attention to every one of the parties cautiously and reaches a resolution which is enthusiastically satisfactory to everything is known as the mediator. A mediator in a perfect world should be unbiased and impartial and ought not lean toward any one. He wants to comprehend what is happening and the parties well and choose something which will help all. It isn't consistently that individuals will effortlessly acknowledge the arbitrator's choice; they might counter it on the off chance that they feel their own advantages are not fulfilled. In such a circumstance, where the moderator is left with no decision, he should utilize his ability to force his thoughts on all, after each of the one can't satisfy everybody. A moderator must be somewhat prudent and brilliant enough to deal with all circumstances and reach to a resolution.

Components of Negotiation

a) Process-The manner in which people haggle with one another is known as the course of exchange. The interaction incorporates the different methods and techniques utilized to arrange and reach to an answer.

b) Behavior-How two parties act with one another during the course of exchange is alluded to as conduct. The manner in which they connect with one another, the manner in which they speak with one another to come to their meaningful conclusions clear totally gone under conduct.

c) Substance-There must be a plan on which people arrange. A point is significant for exchange. In the principal circumstance, going for the late night film was the plan on which you needed to haggle with your folks as well as your companions.

To close, exchange is essentially a strategy, a conversation among people to reach to a common negotiation where everybody acquires something or the other and clashes are kept away from. Negotiation is characterized as a conversation among people to reach to a resolution adequate to the whole gang. It is a cycle where individuals rather than battling among themselves sit together, assess the advantages and disadvantages and afterward emerge with an elective which would be a mutually beneficial negotiation for all. Negotiation helps in lessening clashes and questions among one another. Exchange is fundamental in varying social statuses for a tranquil and peaceful living.

The different models of negotiation:

1. Win Win Model - In this model, every single individual engaged with negotiation wins. No one is at misfortune in this model and each one is benefited out of the exchange. This is the most acknowledged model of negotiation.

2. Win Lose Model - In this model one party successes and the other party loses. In such a model, after a few rounds of conversations and dealings, one party benefits while the party stays disappointed.

3. Lose Lose Model - As the name recommends, in this model, the result of exchange is zero. No party is benefited out of this model. In this model, by and large the two parties are not able to acknowledge each other's perspectives and are hesitant to think twice about. No conversations help.

4. RADPAC Model of Negotiation: RADPAC Model of Negotiation is a generally involved model of negotiation in corporate.

a) R- Rapport: As the name recommends, it implies the connection between parties associated with negotiation. The parties engaged with exchange preferably ought to be alright with one another and share a decent affinity with one another.

b) A - Analysis: One party should comprehend the subsequent party well. The individual must see each other's requirements and interest. The retailer should comprehend the client's necessities and pocket, similarly the client mustn't disregard the businessperson's benefits too. Individuals should pay attention to one another mindfully.

c) D - Debate: Nothing can be accomplished without conversations. This round incorporates examining issues among the parties associated with exchange. The upsides and downsides of a thought are assessed in this round. Individuals banter with one another and every one attempts to persuade the other. One should not blow his top in this round yet keep quiet and made.

d) P - Propose: Each individual proposes his smartest thought in this round. Every one attempts his level best to think of the most ideal thought and reach to a resolution adequate by all.

e) A - Agreement: Individuals arrive at a resolution at this stage and consent to the most ideal other option.

f) C - Close: The exchange is finished and people return back fulfilled.

The exchange between people to arrive at a typical resolution helping everything is called as negotiation. Negotiation alludes to the conversations among people assessing the upsides and downsides of a circumstance and coming to an elective most ideal to all. In negotiation, people attempt their level best to arrive at a resolution which would fulfill all. In less difficult words, it is additionally called as Bargaining. Negotiation happens in different ways in corporates for expanded result and better relations among representatives.

The different negotiations that we go through day by day are as per the following:

a) Day to Day Negotiation at work place-Every day we arrange something or the other at the working environment either with our bosses or with our kindred specialists for the smooth progression of work. These are called everyday negotiations.

b) Negotiation among representative and unrivaled At the work place, a worker needs to haggle with his bosses so he is appointed the obligations according to his inclinations and specialization. Acknowledge nothing you are not happy with. Sit with your chief and examine things with him. How about we guess your supervisor needs you to set up a report on marking and promoting systems of the association and showcasing was never your specialization. Try not to acknowledge it on the grounds that your supervisor has advised you to do as such. Haggle with him, presumably you can cover another subject and another person can be approached to set up the report on promoting and marking. It is smarter to haggle at the primary spot to keep away from clashes and misconceptions later. A person prior to tolerating any deal ought to arrange his compensation with the concerned individual to stay away from pressures later. In the event that you are not getting what you merit, you won't ever partake in your work. Don't simply acknowledge any proposition since you want a task, its fitting all the time to haggle a long time prior to joining any association.

c) Negotiation between associates Negotiation is fundamental among colleagues to diminish the possibilities of debates and clashes. A specific colleague ought not be over troubled while the other part is unwinding. One ought to haggle with his kindred laborers and acknowledge just those obligations he believes he is best equipped for doing. The obligation of accomplishing the objectives ought not lay on just one shoulder, yet similarly split between all. Haggle with your colleagues and acknowledge the obligations readily. To go for a leave for certain, days, haggle with your colleague to deal with your work in your nonattendance. At the point when he disappears, you can help him similarly. Negotiation assists with expanding the result of the group and in the long run the usefulness of the association. Individuals accomplish what they expect and consequently errors and clashes are diminished generally and the workplace improves as a work environment.

d) Commercial exchanges Commercial dealings are by and large done as agreement. Two parties sit eye to eye across the table, examine issues among them and come to conditions adequate to both the parties. In such cases; everything should be clearly. An agreement is endorsed by both the parties and the two of them need to stick to its agreements.

e) Legal Negotiation-Legal negotiation happens among individual and the law where the individual needs to submit to the guidelines and guidelines laid by the general set of laws and the overall set of laws additionally considers the requirements and interest of the person.

Henceforth, dealings are fundamental at work environment so everybody is fulfilled and no body learns about left or ignored. It additionally lessens clashes and mistaken assumptions among individual specialists.

3. What is Conciliation? Elaborate this technique of ADR settlement process. Explain the provisions of conciliation under the Arbitration and Conciliation Act, 1996

Answer

Conciliation is one of the most popular opportunity dispute resolution (ADR) tactics. It allows parties to resolve nearly any dispute using a 3rd-party conciliator. The conciliator gets tasked with resolving differences. Conciliation is a common dispute resolution process. It entails each events concerned in a dispute building a superb relationship. This way, an agreement can take region while not having to go through the USA courtroom system. There are key variations between conciliation, mediation, and arbitration. Conciliation regularly takes place to remedy labor and patron disputes. But humans additionally use it to resolve a wide-form of disagreements. An unbiased conciliator receives tasked with supporting parties in the course of negotiations. He or she directs to the events in the direction of securing a final agreement. Unlike arbitration, conciliation does now not have a recognition for seeming opposed. Conciliation focuses on two key procedures. 1. Recognizing a proper it is violated. 2. Searching to discover a lasting answer. Any conciliation manner revolves round locating the first-class answer for both events. The conciliator focuses on directing the events closer to a common settlement. Think again. Unlike mediators, every conciliator has an instantaneous function in resolving a dispute. He or she provides advice to both parties when it comes to locating answers. The conciliator makes proposals which can cause securing a agreement. The conciliator serves as a impartial third party-party who performs the position of an authority discern. He or she receives tasked with finding the best answer for all parties. The parties do not broaden and suggest agreement terms. Instead, the conciliator conducts those key actions. Parties come to a conciliator once they want direct steerage. That brings up a key difference between conciliation and mediation. A mediator continues a hundred percent impartiality and neutrality always. He or she by no means takes whole obligation for finding lasting solutions. Instead, the mediator works with the events inside the function of a trusted accomplice. This manner, the mediator can help the events in locating a solution. A mediator specializes in facilitating discussions which could lead to an answer. Conciliation and mediation every deal with having the events keep enterprise relationships. Or, the focal point can shift to restoring the balance of strength between the events. The unique processes for those moves fluctuate in mediation and conciliation. Through mediation, your average mediator takes the following steps. 1. Introduction. 2. Holding a joint session. 3. Caucus. 4. Securing a very last settlement. In evaluation, conciliation does now not comply with this well-known system very frequently. Each conciliator uses a wide-type of traditional negotiation strategies. The unique strategies and techniques depend on the specifics of every dispute. Conciliators use many negotiation strategies to discover a lasting answer for the events. Many conciliators assist parties with the aid of having them create a list of all their key desires. These are the capability results that the events wish will come to fruition. Next, the conciliator will have the events rank their particular lists.

The parties will then listing their outcome-dreams from maximum to least essential. The conciliator then has enough cloth to help the parties move from side to side with their desires. He or she can inspire the events to discover not unusual ground that helps a fast resolution. While relating to lists, a conciliator can help the parties construct a string of successes. This way, the events can talk in an surroundings of advanced consider. Keep in thoughts that most conciliators are very professional when it comes to negotiating. Some conciliators opt for not to recognition at the above-cited method of bilateral negotiation. Instead, their undertaking is to apply deep-listening techniques whilst the events speak. This kind of conciliator isn't always that targeted at the events' dreams. Instead, she or he concentrates on helping the events resolve disputes on their personal. A conciliator excels at making sure every birthday party knows wherein the other's coming from. This manner, new and alternative answers can emerge. The conciliator addresses all strength disparities between the events in a comfortable manner. Doing so creates a healthful communicate which could facilitate a decision. This sort of conciliation is non-linear and much less formal than bilateral negotiation. Bilateral negotiation is high-quality for felony problems like tort accidents and property rights. Conciliation is a preventive method to clear up battle. It regularly works first-rate as quickly as a misunderstanding or dispute takes vicinity. Parties bring in a conciliator to prevent conflicts from escalating. Conflicts variety from regulation violations to emotional disputes, along with divorce and separation. Sure, conciliation and arbitration are very distinctive. But there's one key concept that they each have in commonplace. Conciliation and arbitration save you parties from having to spend time/cash on litigation. Mediation can also carry this key gain. Conciliators do now not must go through any general schooling procedure. But many conciliators have sufficient criminal enjoy that may assist resolve disputes. Some conciliators do have special schooling for resolving agency-employee disputes. A conciliator makes a specialty of facilitating verbal exchange among disputing events. He or she steers the events closer to securing a mutual settlement. Conciliators portals difficult to consider the positions of each party. Unlike mediators, conciliators can offer evaluations related to the merits of every argument. Then, they are able to recommend a truthful final results or agreement phrases. Arbitration is a proper kind of alternative dispute decision (ADR). It functions arbitral tribunal techniques wherein selections get determined through arbitrators, also referred to as Arbitration Decision. Conciliation and mediation feature much less formal techniques. They both attention on facilitating communication between the disputing events. This way, disputes can get resolved without the want to visit litigation. Conciliators use evaluative methods and provide hints. But Mediators do not make proposals for agreement. Through mediation, a third party neutral assists in resolving a dispute. Meanwhile, conciliators recognition on resolving disputes on a more direct foundation. Conciliation is a not unusual shape of the complete dispute decision method. It includes a conciliator establishing a superb relationship with all disputing parties. That is one key difference between conciliation and mediation or arbitration. Through conciliation, the parties do no longer expand and advise phrases of a settlement. Instead, the conciliator does so after assembly to the events. The intention of any conciliation proceeding is to clear up a dispute. Conciliation resolutions are frequently fast, amicable, and value-efficient. Another key motive of conciliation is for the events to avoid US court litigation. That is one main reason why conciliation regularly saves events a whole lot of cash. There are two not unusual kinds of conciliation on the subject of dispute resolution. There is civil conciliation and domestic conciliation. Civil conciliation refers to settling small court cases in a inexpensive manner than litigation. Domestic litigation refers to emotional disputes. As an example, a couple working out terms of a divorce may want to benefit through conciliation.

PROVISIONS OF CONCILIATION UNDER THE ACT OF 1996

Section 61 of the Arbitration and Conciliation Act of 1996 provides for the Application and Scope of Conciliation which points out that the process of conciliation extends, in the first place, to disputes, whether contractual or not and they must arise out of the legal relationship. In a dispute, one party has the right to sue and to the other party the liability to be sued. But Part III of the Act does not apply to such disputes.

Section 63 of the Act fixes the number of conciliators. Ideally only 1 conciliator is required but the parties may by their agreement provide for two or three conciliators.

Appointment of a conciliator

According to Section 64 of the Arbitration and conciliation Act, 1996-

(1) Subject to sub-section-

(a) in conciliation proceedings with one conciliator, the parties may agree on the name of a sole conciliator;

(b) in conciliation proceedings with two conciliators, each party may appoint one conciliator;

(c) in conciliation proceedings with three conciliators, each party may appoint one conciliator and the parties may agree on the name of the third conciliator who shall act as the presiding conciliator.

(2) Parties may enlist the assistance of a suitable institution or person in connection with the appointment of conciliators, and in particular,

(a) a party may request such an institution or person to recommend the names of suitable individuals to act as conciliator; or

(b) the parties may agree that the appointment of one or more conciliators be made directly by such an institution or person.

The parties have to agree on the composition of the conciliation tribunal when the invitation to conciliation is acknowledged. In the absence of any agreement to the contrary, there shall be only one conciliator. If both the parties fail to appoint a conciliator with consent, same may be conducted by two conciliators (maximum limit is three), then each party appoints own conciliator, and the third conciliator is appointed unanimously by both the parties. The third conciliator so designated shall be the directing conciliator. The gatherings to the discretion understanding as opposed to selecting the conciliator themselves may enroll the help of an organization or individual of their decision for arrangement of conciliators. In any case, the establishment or the individual should keep in view during arrangement that, the conciliator is free and unbiased.

Role of the conciliator

Section 67 of the act describes the role of conciliator as-

(1) The conciliator shall assist the parties in an independent and impartial manner in their attempt to reach an amicable settlement of their dispute.

(2) The conciliator shall be guided by principles of objectivity, fairness and justice, giving consideration to, among other things, the rights and obligations of the parties, the usages of the trade concerned and the circumstances surrounding the dispute, including any previous business practices between the parties.

(3) The conciliator may conduct the conciliation proceedings in such a manner as he considers appropriate, taking into account the circumstances of the case, the wishes the parties may express, including any request by a

party that the conciliator hear oral statements, and the need for a speedy settlement of the dispute.

(4) The conciliator may, at any stage of the conciliation proceedings, make proposals for a settlement of the dispute. Such proposals need not be writing and need not be accompanied by a statement of the reasons therefore.

A conciliator is also expected to review relevant documents and information to help reach conclusions. Meet with witnesses and other persons related to the parties to obtain statements and additional information about the dispute in question and practice confidentiality regarding the personal information of the parties and of the dispute. A brief written statement of all the issues faced by the parties is to be submitted to the conciliator before the process of conciliation. A positive dialogue and an atmosphere of comfort is to be created by the conciliator in order to promote a harmonious and cooperative problem solving between the parties. In India conciliator plays an evaluative role where he attempts to get the gatherings to acknowledge the benefits and demerits of their cases along these lines driving them to a general adequate arrangement. Along with being well educated a conciliator should impact the parties with his/her personal and convincing skills and playa proactive role in reaching an agreement.

Restrictions on Role of Conciliator

Section 80 places two restrictions on the role of the conciliator in the conduct of conciliation proceedings:

1. Clause (a) prohibits the conciliator to act as an arbitrator or as a representative or counsel of a party in any arbitral or judicial proceeding in respect of a dispute which is subject of the conciliation proceedings.
2. Clause (b) of prohibits the parties to produce the conciliator as a witness in any arbitral or judicial proceedings.

Commencement of conciliator proceedings

Either of the parties to the dispute can commence the conciliation process. The conciliation proceedings are said to have been initiated, when one party invites the other party for resolution of their dispute through conciliation. The process commences when the other party accepts the invitation. If they reject it, then no conciliation proceedings will be conducted for that dispute. The invitation should identify the subject of the dispute. If no reply is received by the inviting party within 30 days then it may be treated as rejection to conciliate.

Commencement of conciliation proceedings under section 62 of the act states that-

(1) The party initiating conciliation shall send to the other party a written invitation to conciliate under this Part, briefly identifying the subject of the dispute.

(2) Conciliation proceedings shall commence when the other party accepts in writing the invitation to conciliate.

(3) If the other party rejects the invitation, there will be no conciliation proceedings.

(4) If the party initiating conciliation does not receive a reply within thirty days from the date on which he sends the invitation, or within such other period of time as specified in the invitation, he may elect to treat this as a rejection of the invitation to conciliate and if he so elects, he shall inform in writing the other party accordingly.

The conciliation proceedings shall be terminated as given under section 76-

(a) by the signing of the settlement agreement by the parties on the date of the agreement; or

(b) by a written declaration of the conciliator, after consultation with the parties, to the effect that further efforts at conciliation are no longer justified, on the date of the declaration; or

(c) by a written declaration of the parties addressed to the conciliator to the effect that the conciliation proceedings are terminated, on the date of the declaration; or

(d) by a written declaration of a party to the other party and the conciliator, if appointed, to the effect that the conciliation proceedings are terminated, on the date of the declaration.

The conciliation proceedings shall stand terminated on the date as and when the parties reach an amicable settlement on the disputes which had been referred to the conciliator, and a duly authenticated copy (by the conciliator) of the settlement agreement is handed over to the parties. There is no provision in the Act for review of the settlement agreement, nor there does any provision under which any of the parties to the settlement agreement can retrace its steps and wriggle out of the written commitments in the form of a settlement agreement.

Principle of confidentiality

In a conciliation proceeding, two parties resolve the matter and confidentiality is something which is guaranteed by the statute itself which makes it one of the highlighting features of alternative dispute resolution. In conciliation, both the parties and the conciliator are obligatory to keep the facts and all the material relating to the proceedings very confidential. Details and opinions/views of other parties is not to be discussed by the parties in respect of the possible settlement of their dispute. They should also refrain from making admission of other parties and other conciliators in the course of the proceedings. Matters regarding the dispute is required not to speak about any information or not to bring out any e subject matter regarding the dispute to other party or conciliators during the cancellation process. During the proceedings, a conciliator can never play the role of a witness.

Section 75 describes Confidentiality as: Notwithstanding anything contained in any other law for the time being in force, the conciliator and the parties shall keep confidential all matters relating to the conciliation proceedings. Confidentiality shall extend also to the settlement agreement, except where its disclosure is necessary for purposes of implementation and enforcement.

In the case of Haresh Dayaram Thakur v. State of Maharashtra and Ors. AIR 2000 SC 2281, While dealing with the provisions of Sections 73 and 74 of the Arbitration and Conciliation Act of 1996 in paragraph 19 of the judgment as expressed thus the court held that from the statutory provisions noted above the position is manifest that a conciliator is a person who is to assist the parties to settle the disputes between them amicably. For this purpose the conciliator is vested with wide powers to decide the procedure to be followed by him untrammelled by the procedural law like the Code of Civil Procedure or the Indian Evidence Act, 1872. When the parties are able to resolve the dispute between them by mutual agreement and it appears to the conciliator that their exists an element of settlement which may be acceptable to the parties he is to proceed in accordance with the procedure laid down in Section 73. It follows therefore that a successful conciliation proceeding comes to end only when the settlement agreement signed by the parties comes into existence. It is such an agreement which has the status and effect of legal sanctity of an arbitral award under Section 74.

The process of conciliation as an alternate dispute redressal mechanism is beneficial to the parties as it is expeditious and cost effective which makes it simple compared to the lengthy litigation. However, the success of conciliation depends on the attitude of the parties, the skill of the conciliator and the appropriate environment, backed by infrastructure facilities for servicing the conciliation procedure. On ultimate analytical observation, reciprocity is the hallmark of conciliation process. Mutual understanding is required for healthy business and to solve the dispute through settlement are the eventual qualities or eventual base as it leads to success in conciliation. In contrast to arbitration, conciliation is nonbonding and confidential. The court plays no formal role in sponsoring conciliation.

Conciliation is becoming increasingly popular, as an alternative to other formal and informal modes of dispute resolution as it offers a more flexible alternative, for a wide variety of disputes and obviates the parties from seeking recourse to the court system. It also reserves the freedom of the parties to withdraw from conciliation without prejudice to their legal position inter se at any stage of the proceedings. Conciliation is a boon and it is a better procedure to settle any dispute as in this process it is the parties who by themselves only come to the settlement of the dispute and it tries to individualize the optimal solution and direct parties towards a satisfactory common agreement.

CHAPTER FOUR

LOK ADALATS AND THE LEGAL SERVICES AUTHORITIES

1. What do you mean by Lok Adalat? Explain the origin of Lok Adalats.

Answer

The idea of Lok Adalat (People's Court) is a modern Indian contribution to the world jurisprudence. The advent of Lok Adalats introduced a new bankruptcy to the justice dispensation gadget of this system and succeeded in imparting a supplementary forum to the sufferers for a exceptional settlement of their disputes. This gadget is based totally on Gandhian concepts. It is one of the components of ADR (Alternative Dispute Resolution) structures. In ancient instances, the disputes have been noted "Panchayats", which have been hooked up on the village level. Panchayats resolved the disputes via arbitration. It has proved to be a totally powerful alternative to litigation.

This concept of the agreement of disputes thru mediation, negotiation or arbitration is conceptualized and institutionalized within the philosophy of Lok Adalat. It involves folks who are immediately or circuitously affected by dispute resolution.

Origin of Lok Adalats

The concept of Lok Adalats changed into pushed returned into oblivion in previous couple of centuries earlier than independence and in particular all through the British regime. Now, this concept has, yet again, been rejuvenated. It has become very famous and acquainted amongst litigants.

This is the system, which has deep roots in Indian criminal records and its close allegiance to the subculture and perception of justice in Indian ethos. Experience has shown that it is one of the very green and important

ADR mechanisms and maximum suitable to the Indian surroundings, subculture and societal hobbies. Camps of Lok Adalats had been started initially in Gujarat in March 1982 and now it has been prolonged all through the Country.

The evolution of this motion becomes a part of the strategy to relieve heavy burden at the Courts with pending instances and to give comfort to the litigants. The first Lok Adalat became hung on March 14, 1982 at Junagarh in Gujarat. Maharashtra began the Lok Nyayalaya in 1984.

The introduction of Legal Services Authorities Act, 1987 gave a statutory repute to Lok Adalats, pursuant to the constitutional mandate in Article 39-A of the Constitution of India. It consists of numerous provisions for settlement of disputes through Lok Adalat.

This Act mandates constitution of felony offerings government to provide loose and able prison services to the weaker sections of the society and to ensure that opportunities for securing justice aren't denied to any citizen by way of reason of economic or different disabilities.

It additionally mandates organisation of Lok Adalats to steady that the operation of the felony system promotes justice on the premise of identical possibility. When statutory reputation had been given to Lok Adalat, it was particularly furnished that the award exceeded by using the Lok Adalat formulating the terms of compromise could have the pressure of decree of a courtroom, which can be carried out as a civil court docket decree.

The evolution of movement known as Lok Adalat changed into a part of the strategy to alleviate heavy burden at the Courts with pending instances and to give alleviation to the litigants who have been in a queue to get justice. It incorporates various provisions for agreement of disputes through Lok Adalat.

The events aren't allowed to be represented by way of the attorneys and recommended to interact with choose who facilitates in arriving at amicable agreement. No price is paid through the parties. Strict rule of Civil Procedural Court and evidence isn't implemented. Decision is with the aid of casual sitting and binding at the parties and no enchantment lies against the order of the Lok Adalat.

2. What do you mean by Permanent Lok Adalat?

Answer

In 2002, the Parliament added about sure amendments to the Legal Services Authorities Act, 1987 to institutionalize the Lok Adalats by means of making them a everlasting body to settle the disputes associated with public utility offerings. The Central or State Authorities might also, through notification, establish Permanent Lok Adalats at any Permanent Lok Adalats, for determining troubles in connection to Public Utility Services. Public Services encompass: Transport service, Postal, telegraph or smartphone services, Supply of power, light and water to public, System of public conservancy or sanitation, Insurance offerings and such other offerings as notified with the aid of the Central or State Governments. Permanent Lok Adalats have the equal powers which might be vested inside the Lok Adalats.

3. Throw light on the jurisdiction of Lok Adalats.

Answer

A Lok Adalat shall have jurisdiction to determine and to reach at a compromise or agreement among the parties to a dispute in admire of: any case pending earlier than; or any be counted which is falling within the jurisdiction of, and is not added before, any courtroom for which the Lok Adalat is organized. The Lok Adalat can compromise and settle even criminal cases, which are compoundable beneath the applicable laws.

4. What are the cases that the Lok Adalat can deal with?

Answer

Lok Adalats can deal with the following cases:

a. Compoundable civil, revenue and criminal cases

b. Motor accident compensation claims cases

c. Partition Claims

d. Damages Cases

e. Matrimonial and family disputes

f. Mutation of lands case

g. Land Pattas cases

h. Bonded Labor cases

i. Land acquisition disputes

j. Bank's unpaid loan cases.

k. Arrears of retirement benefits cases

l. Family Court cases

m. Cases, which are not subjudice.

5. Examine the provisions of ADR under Legal Services Authority Act, 1987.

OR

Explain Lok Adalats as an method of Alternative Dispute Resolution.

Answer

The literal meaning of Lok Adalat is People's Court. It has defined as a forum where voluntary effort is aimed at bringing about settlement of disputes between the parties is made through conciliatory and persuasive means.

It is an ADR forum that not only minimizes expenses on litigation, but it saves valuable time of the parties and their witness and facilitates settlement to the satisfaction of the parties. India is a democratic country and the rule of law is the guiding principle of administration of justice ensuring equality before of law and equal protection of law under Article 14 of the Constitution of India to all the citizens is the constitutional obligation of the state.

The Preamble to the Constitution provides for securing for all citizens justice – social, political, economic and equality of opportunity. The Directive Principles of State Policy (DPSP) under Art. 39-A also mandates that the State shall ensure that the operation of the legal system promotes justice on the basis of equal opportunity and in particular provide free legal aid, by suitable legislation or scheme and ensure that opportunity for securing justice is not denied to any citizen by reason of economic or other disabilities.

In the case of Hussainaira Khatoon v. Home Secretary, State of Bihar (AIR 1970), the apex court held that the concept of legal aid and speedy trials are an integral part of right to life and liberty under Article 21 of the constitution of India.

In the case of State of Maharasthra v. Manu Bhai Bagaji Vashi (AIR 1995), the apex court held that to ensure that free legal aid is available to the needy, poor and that the State should initiate measures to organize paralegal services and legal literacy programs throughout the country.

THE LEGAL SERVICES AUTHORITY ACT, 1987

Art. 39A of the constitution of India was added via 42nd Constitutional Amendment Act, 1976 which casts an obligation on the state to provide free legal aid to the indigent persons and to provide opportunity so as to secure justice for all are not denied to any citizen by way of economic or other disabilities. With a view to accomplish this objective, the government of India appointed a committee for implementing legal aid scheme in 1980 headed by Justice P N Bhagwati. The Committee prepared a draft legal aid which could be applied throughout India. On the basis of the recommendation of the outline of this Committee, the Legal Services Authority Act, 1987 was passed to establish statutory legal services authorities. It also contained provisions relating to the Lok Adalats.

OBJECTIVE OF THE ACT

The main objectives of the Act are:

a. To provide free and competent legal services to the poor and the weaker sections of the society,
b. To ensure that they are not denied opportunity of securing justice by reason of economic or other disabilities, and
c. To organize the Lok Adalats to secure that the opportunity of the legal system promotes justice on the basis of equal opportunity.

The Act of 1987 owes its origin to Art. 39A of the constitution of India was passed by the Parliament with a view to ensure free and competent legal aid services to the weaker sections of the society so that they are not denied of opportunities for securing justice by reason of economic or other disabilities.

In keeping the view of the elgal philosophy envisaged under the constitutional provisions providing legal assistance to the poor and needy, the legal services comes as a boon for the indigent persons.

In the case of Ellanath Sahu v. State (1990), the Orissa High Court observed that free legal aid at the state cost is a fundamental right of a person accused of an offence which may involve jeopardy to his life or personal liberty and this is the fundamental right which is implicit under Article 21 of the constitution of India.

ENTITLEMENT OF LEGAL SERVICES

Sec. 13 of the Act of 1987 provides that persons who satisfy all or any of the criteria specified u/s 12 shall be entitled to avail legal services provided that the concerned legal aid authority is satisfied that such person has a prima facie to prosecute or defend.

ORGANIZATION OF LOK ADALATS

Lok Adalats are judicial bodies set up for the purpose of facilitating peaceful resolution of disputes between the litigating parties. They have the powers of an ordinary court civil in nature such as summoning, examining, taking evidence etc. These Adalats can resolve the matters except criminal cases that are non-compoundable in nature.

Sec. 19 of the Act provides that every Central. State or District Legal Services Authority or the Supreme Court Legal Services Committee or the High Court Legal Services Committee as the case may be, shall organize lok adalats at such intervals and at places and for exercising jurisdiction and for such areas as it may deem fit.

Every lok adalat organized for an area shall consist of:-

a. A sitting or a retired judicial officer, and
b. Other persons of repute as may be prescribed by the state authority or district authority or Supreme Court legal Services Committee or the High Court Legal Services Committee or as the case may be, the Taluka Legal Services Committee organizing the Lok Adalats.

The qualifications and experience prescribed for these persons for lok adalats organized by the Supreme Court Legal Service Committee shall be as such deemed fit by the Central Government in consultation with the Chief Justice of India.

Rule 13 of National Legal Services Authority Rules provides that a person shall not be qualified as to be included as a member of the lok adalat unless he is:

a. A member of legal profession,
b. A person of repute who is specially interested in the implementation of the legal services scheme and programs, or
c. An eminent social worker who is engaged in the upliftment of weaker sections of the people including the SCs, STs, women, children, rural and urban labor.

Sec. 19(4) of the Act of 1987 provides that the experience and qualifications of other persons as mentioned earlier or lok adalats other than those which are prescribed by the central government in consultation with the Chief justice of the supreme court shall be such as may be prescribed by the state government in consultation with the Chief Justices of the concerned High Courts.

In the case of Public Prosecutor, High Court of Andhra Pradesh v. Basireddy Verma Reddy (AIR 2009) it was held that lok Adalat is not equated to the court for the purpose of Sec. 320(2) of Cr.P.C., 1973 which relates to the compounding of offences. Lok Adalat is not an adjudicatory body for the simple reason is that it is meant to resolve the disputes by invoking any one of the suitable modes under the ADR mechanism.

CHAPTER FIVE

ARBITRATION

Q1. What is arbitration? What are the merits and demerits of arbitration?

Answer

WIPO defines arbitration as "Arbitration is a procedure in which a dispute is submitted, by agreement of the parties, to one or more arbitrators who make a binding decision on the dispute. In choosing arbitration, the parties opt for a private dispute resolution procedure instead of going to court."

Its principal characteristics are:

a. Arbitration is consensual: Arbitration can only take place if both parties have agreed to it. In the case of future disputes arising under a contract, the parties insert an arbitration clause in the relevant contract. An existing dispute can be referred to arbitration by means of a submission agreement between the parties. In contrast to mediation, a party cannot unilaterally withdraw from arbitration.

b. The parties choose the arbitrator(s): Under the WIPO Arbitration Rules, the parties can select a sole arbitrator together. If they choose to have a three-member arbitral tribunal, each party appoints one of the arbitrators; those two persons then agree on the presiding arbitrator. Alternatively, the Center can suggest potential arbitrators with relevant expertise or directly appoint members of the arbitral tribunal. The Center maintains an extensive roster of arbitrators ranging from seasoned dispute-resolution generalists to highly specialized practitioners and experts covering the entire legal and technical spectrum of intellectual property.

c. Arbitration is neutral: In addition to their selection of neutrals of appropriate nationality, parties are able to choose such important elements as the applicable law, language and venue of the arbitration. This allows them to ensure that no party enjoys a home court advantage.

d. Arbitration is a confidential procedure: The WIPO Rules specifically protect the confidentiality of the existence of the arbitration, any disclosures made during that procedure, and the award. In certain circumstances, the WIPO Rules allow a party to restrict access to trade secrets or other confidential information that is submitted to the arbitral tribunal or to a confidentiality advisor to the tribunal.

e. The decision of the arbitral tribunal is final and easy to enforce: Under the WIPO Rules, the parties agree to carry out the decision of the arbitral tribunal without delay. International awards are enforced by national courts under the New York Convention, which permits them to be set aside only in very limited circumstances. More than 165 States are party to this Convention.

Q2. What are the advantages and disadvantages of arbitration?
Answer

ADVANTAGES OF ARBITRATION

a. Cost successful: In assertion, not much legitimate readiness is required. A large portion of the charges or expenses caused during the assertion interaction are split between both the gatherings. This makes this cycle a lot less expensive than the conventional case.

b. Simple and casual strategy: In assertion, the gatherings don't need to enlist backers to address them. The gatherings would themselves be able to introduce their issues and requests before the authority. No proper idiosyncrasies are utilized in this cycle which brings about an agreeable climate.

c. Fairness: In conventional legitimate preliminary, neither one of the parts can pick the adjudicator who will choose their case. Be that as it may, in assertion, both the gatherings have the freedom to pick judge. This outcomes in a fair result.

d. Efficient and adaptable: The conventional prosecution invests in some opportunity to determine. It might likewise take more time to tackle a specific case. A lawful goal through discretion is much speedier than prosecution. Intervention is more adaptable regarding booking. Assertion hearings can advantageously be planned in view of the accessibility of gatherings and the mediator.

e. Convenience: In prosecution, the date of hearing is still up in the air by the Court. For this, the comfort of the gatherings isn't remembered. Here and there, the gatherings need to trust that lengthy timespan will get trials. Be that as it may, in assertion, parties reserve the privilege to concur upon a specific date as appropriate for themselves as well as their observers.

f. Confidentiality: In Court, every one of the procedures are available to public. Be that as it may, in intervention, any divulgence made by the gatherings in the procedures is to be kept private. Consequently, the assertion legitimate interaction is more private than prosecution.

g. Finality: The choice made by the referee is last one. There isn't any arrangement of allure in the assertion interaction.

h. Agreeableness: In assertion, neither party wins nor misfortunes. Both the gatherings came to a pleasant result which is in consistence with their requirements.

i. Full control of the interaction: Both the gatherings have every one of the privileges to decide by understanding the direct of the procedures.

DISADVANTAGES OF ARBITRATION

Each coin has different sides. Alongside various benefits, there are various burdens of mediation that the gatherings ought to remember whether they need to go for assertion. The significant ones among them are as per the following:

a. No Appeals: The choice given by the referee is considered as last. There is no arrangement of allure in mediation process. Regardless of whether one party feels that the result of assertion process was unreasonable, out of line, or one-sided, they don't have the choice to pursue it.

b. Cost: Arbitration is for the most part considered as a practical cycle when contrasted with case. Be that as it may, this element holds no importance in those cases in which insignificant cash is involved.

c. Rules of Evidence: In a Court of regulation, an adjudicator needs to adhere to explicit guidelines and guidelines while tolerating proof. Be that as it may, it isn't the case in intervention. Judges can use any data that is brought to them.

d. Limited powers of referee: The Court has the ability to rebuff the defendants who are obstructive or lazy in their direct of the procedures. In any case, an authority's powers are not so solid as to track down somebody in disdain of court.

e. Questionable Fairness in Mandatory intervention: If the actual agreement expresses that mediation is compulsory in the event that any question emerges then the gatherings don't have the adaptability to pick discretion upon shared assent.

f. Lack of straightforwardness: The intervention hearings are for the most part not made open to public and are held in private. This can be a positive as well as a negative element of mediation. This absence of straightforwardness might transform the cycle one-sided and eventually result into treachery.

g. Inconsistently keeping the law: Although it is correct that the judge needs to observe the law yet the principles are not satisfactory. It is exceptionally conceivable that the referee might consider the "obvious decency" of the individual gatherings' situations rather than rigorously keeping the law. This turns out to be more huge when our party would be inclined toward by a severe use of the law.

Q3. What is arbitration agreement? What are the essentials of arbitration agreement?

Answer

The gatherings are by and large expected to consent to an Arbitration Arrangement. The choice taken by the authority with respect to any issue, is restricting on both the gatherings, as expressed by the understanding. Regardless, where one party concludes that an arrangement should be made before entering the agreement, it very well may be expressed that the understanding was made to go amiss from the issues of the court. These arrangements resemble contingent agreements, and that implies that these arrangements will possibly come into force or become enforceable assuming any debate occurs, and based on similar question between two gatherings referenced in the agreement. It likewise happens or is enforceable in the radiance of any debate that emerges between the gatherings to the agreement.

Basics of an Arbitration Agreement

a) There should be a question that ought to occur, really at that time the arrangement will be legitimate. The presence of a debate among the gatherings is a fundamental condition for the agreement to occur. At the point when the gatherings have resolved the question, for no situation, they can conjure the discretion proviso to disprove the settlement.

b) Another fundamental is the composed understanding. An understanding connected with the intervention should generally be recorded as a hard copy. A discretion arrangement will be considered as a composed understanding when:

1. It hosts been endorsed by the two gatherings and it is as an archive

2. It can be the trading of the message, the letters, the wires, or some other method for correspondence which gives the record of the trade and the arrangement for assertion

3. There should be a trade of proclamations between the gatherings that gives the assertion of case and protection in which the presence of the understanding of the discretion is concurred by one of the gatherings and which isn't characterized by the other party.

c) The third fundamental goal. The goal of the gatherings while framing the agreement is of most extreme significance and it shapes the premise of the understanding. There have been no essential references of terms, for example, an "authority" or "mediation" to be settled on in the arrangement. Subsequently, it is important to take note of that the aim of the two players assumes a vital part in such an understanding. Notwithstanding, one should remember that regardless of whether the words have not been referenced, the expectation should show that both the gatherings have consented to come to the terms with the Arbitration Agreement.

d) The fourth fundamental component is the mark of the gatherings. The mark of the gatherings is a fundamental component to comprise a discretion understanding. The mark can be as a record endorsed by both the gatherings to the agreement which involves every one of the agreements, or it can likewise be as an archive which is endorsed by just a single party to the agreement which contains the terms and acknowledgment by the other party to the agreement. It will be adequate assuming one party sets up a mark in the arrangement and the other party acknowledges that.

In the milestone instance of K.K. Modi v. K.N. Modi and Ors. (1998) 3 SCC 573, it was held by the Hon'ble Supreme Court that the accompanying credits should be available in a mediation arrangement:

1. The understanding should express that the choice of the court will tie upon by both the gatherings.
2. That the purview of the council on the privileges of the gatherings ought to be chosen by both the gatherings consensually or from a request got by the Court which expresses that the procedure will be made through intervention.
3. The council has the privilege to decide the freedoms of the gatherings by being fair and just.
4. The arrangement that the gatherings will allude to the council should be enforceable by regulation.

e. The arrangement should express that any choice made by the court on the question should be figured out before when the reference is made.

A few normal components remembered for the Agreement other than the fundamental arrangements

Coming up next are a portion of the normal components remembered for a discretion arrangement, which is by and large not considered as a fundamental component, however will be incorporated assuming the gatherings believe that it should be referenced in the agreement.

1. Seat of Arbitration: The seat here implies the spot. Subsequently, this provision expresses that there will be a position of discretion on account of the question. This arrangement is a significant one, particularly on account of a global business assertion, as this seat helps in deciding the procedural regulations that administer the methodology of the mediation. In any case, the seat of the discretion doesn't need to be similar spot as the knowing about the procedures. It is where the assertion happens, despite the fact that it contrasts from the spot of the hearings.

2. Procedure for delegating the Arbitrators: The technique is equivalent to referenced in the Arbitration Act. It expresses that any individual, independent of the ethnicity, might be selected as an authority, except if the gatherings consent to something in any case. The gatherings would themselves be able to concur for the arrangement of an authority.

3. Language: The language assumes a significant part while settling on an arrangement. It is essential that the language which has been picked in the agreement doesn't need to be the one that isn't perceived by the two players. There should not be any kind of correspondence hole and that the understanding made by the gatherings are of such a way that every single condition referenced in the agreement is really perceived by both the gatherings marking the agreement. Picking the language which can be perceived by the two players is significant on the grounds that then it would save both the gatherings, the expense of an interpreter.

4. Number and Qualifications of Arbitrators: The Act permits the gatherings to decide the quantity of the authorities, with the main condition that the number will not be a much number, yet an odd number of mediators, so the choice can be made regardless of whether there is a conflict among the judges.

5. Type of Arbitration: The gatherings have the decision to pick between the institutional and the impromptu (and that implies it is made for that particular reason) sort of discretion. Institutional implies that consenting to be limited by the guidelines of the mediation foundations specially appointed implies that the actual gatherings consent to organize a judge.

6. **Governing Law**: It is essential to make reference to the meaningful regulation that they need to be administered by as neglecting to specify this considerable regulation may be a gigantic issue later on debates emerging between the gatherings, if any.

Important provisions in the arbitration agreement

There are a couple of significant arrangements under a discretion understanding, and these are referenced beneath:

1. Written Agreement: As expressed as a fundamental condition, there should be a composed arrangement. Section 7(4) of the Act, expresses that each arrangement made should be as a composed report or even as any sort of correspondence if those interchanges occur through wires, message or considerably other telecom gadgets given that there should be a record of the correspondence.

2. Appointment of the Arbitrators: Section 11 expresses that the referee can be delegated at the freedom of the gatherings to the agreement. On the off chance that, where the gatherings neglect to choose the arrangement of the mediator, the Chief Justice of the High Court, if there should be an occurrence of the homegrown assertion and the Chief Justice of the Supreme Court, in the event of International Commercial Arbitration is drawn closer.

3. Interim Relief: Section 9 and Section 17 of the Act accommodate the Interim help orders regarding the mediation. The relief request is viable under area 9 assuming there is at first sight proof that there is an arrangement for the discretion continuing. The gatherings, in the event that they need, can move to the Court before the assertion continuing really begins or even subsequent to making the arbitral honor however before its authorization according to section 36 of the Act. Area 17 expresses that, at the gatherings' solicitation, the court might arrange the party to go to between time lengths, the manner in which it considers fit and significant in regard to the topic of the debate.

4. Finality of an Award by Arbitration: Section 34 states that the honor given by the authority is conclusive and is restricting upon the gatherings who have marked the agreement. When the announcement is allowed by the court, it will be enforceable concerning section 34 of the Act.

5. Appeal: Section 37 states that in the event that the gatherings are not happy with the choice of the referees, an allure lies against the request conceding or declining to give any action under area 9 and furthermore against declining to save or saving an honor. An allure can likewise lie against the request for the council tolerating the supplication alluded to in section 16 or giving or declining to allow an interval measure under section 17. Notwithstanding, there is no arrangement for an allure against the arrangement of a judge as given under section 11.

The development of assertion connotes that there is a crucial change that is available in our approach to enacting. Another importance is in concluding the issues in an altogether lesser measure of time and the unique or the different provisos referenced in the business contract. These are preparing for the best and the most reasonable cure without going through the response of the courts. Assertion is by and large the most proficient type of solution for settlement of debates among the gatherings, which really requires no lengthy techniques of the Court for the choices to be made. It is cost-proficient, the time has come saving, it additionally allows one to pick their own judges. Through this, the choices are given quickly, and as per the idea of the case, they are additionally, more often than not acceptable. The severability, distinguishableness, and the independence standard of the Arbitral understanding keep the legitimacy of one arrangement from being covered by the other. Regardless, the two arrangements may exist together. Having such a guideline doesn't refute the worth of different standards referenced in the agreement, yet for the most part adds on to those standards. Hence it assumes a significant part when the legally binding conditions emerge while managing the debates.

Consequently, from the above article, we can express that a discretion arrangement isn't simply advantageous to the gatherings while saving the assets, yet additionally in method for the time and endeavors put in by every one of the gatherings. Notwithstanding a couple of individuals expressing that it's anything but a total procedural part of managing the cases, one express that it assists both the gatherings who with having confronted the debate. Nonetheless, above all, it is vital that there are sure things that must be kept in one's brain before really drafting or while drafting an agreement for the assertion understanding. Practically speaking however, practically all intervention arrangements are closed with assertion provisos.

Q4. Discuss about the interim relief provisions under the Arbitration Act of 1996.

Answer

Section 9 and Section 17 of the Arbitration and Conciliation Act, 1996 give interval relief to the gatherings in mediation. The need for interim measures emerged as, on a few events, conditions emerged where both of the gatherings occupied with exercises that postponed procedures or biased the privileges of different gatherings or turned the judgment in support of themselves. A model for this would auction the contested resource. Between time reliefs fluctuate as indicated by winning circumstances and conditions. Accordingly, to shield the freedoms of the gatherings, an arrangement for giving between time help turned into a need. While both the Sections 9 and 17 of the Act accommodate giving of interimreliefs, the conditions in which they can be benefited fluctuate.

Section 9 of the Act expresses that a party can look for interval measures or assurance from "the Court" previously, later or during the procedures or whenever subsequent to making of the arbitral honor however before its implementation. When the arbitral council has been established, a party will move toward the arbitral court except if the court observes that the overarching conditions don't deliver the cure given by the arbitral council (under Section 17 of the Act) adequate. The words "the Court will not engage" of S. 9 (3) of the Act clarifies that the courts will not give help once the arbitral council has been comprised. On account of Sri Tufan Chatterjee v. Sri Rangan Dhar, the court expressed that "will not engage" stage actually intended that "a party that has the ability to found a procedure under Section 9 at any crossroads, since the word utilized was "engage " and not "foundation " as utilized in Section 3 of the Limitation Act, 1963 (Bar of constraint), the Court is bared of its ability to hear an application on merits except if it is persuaded that the cure under Section 17 isn't solid."

The court can concede interval measures under Section 9 provided that the actions given by the arbitral council are not adequate. Then again, Section 17 of the Act expresses that a party can look for interim measures or security from "the Arbitral Tribunal" during the arbitral procedures or whenever after the creation of the arbitral honor yet before it is implemented. The arbitral council has the very power as that of the court for making orders, with the end goal of, and according to, any procedures before it. Both the sections likewise accommodate the arrangement of a watchman for a minor and unstable individual for arbitral procedures.

While it appears to be that both the courts and councils have a similar ability to concede interval reliefs, the court has more ability to allow help. A plain scrutiny of Section 9 (3) will uncover that the Court has been given a prevalent status than the Arbitral Tribunal. While an inefficacious interval help from the council is a ground to move toward the court, there is no arrangement that gives grounds to move toward the arbitral council in the event of an inefficacious between time relief by a Court. Before the 2015 Amendment Act, interval measures conceded under Section 9 were more than the reliefs allowed in Section 17. Through the 2015 Amendment Act, more power was conceded to the court. The request for a Tribunal was to be considered as a request for court for all reasons and will be implemented in a similar way as a Court request. This was done as S. 9 of the Act was the favored choice for the gatherings even after the Tribunal was established. In this way, with time, the power of arbitral councils is expanding.

There are conditions where there is a cross-over between Sections 9 and 17 of the Act. The Delhi High Court held that a pendency of an application under area 17 doesn't remove the powers of the court to provide request for interim relief. The Andhra Pradesh High Court held that cure under Section 9 of the Act isn't banned regardless of whether it is now, incompletely or completely looked for under Section 17 of the Act. The court is higher in the order and has power, taking everything into account. From this, one might say that the gatherings have two choices. Yet, does this imply that an individual can straightforwardly move toward the court under Section 9? Section 9 (3) expresses that once the council has been set, the court will not engage any application made under s. 9 (1) except if the cure under S. 17 is inefficacious. The court will then, at that point, first analyze the relief conceded under S.17, prior to taking up the case as the council has previously been set. This implies that the party should move toward the council first.

This has been very much made sense of on account of M Ashraf v. Kasim VK. The court gave three phases. The principal stage is before the initiation of arbitral procedures. In this stage, S. 9 (3) of the Act doesn't make a difference. The second is the point at which the arbitral procedures have started. At this stage, it is essential for S. 9 (3) of the demonstration to be fulfilled. The third stage is the point at which the arbitral honor has been made however is yet to be upheld. It is to be noticed that at this stage, the council has stopped to work. Besides in cases gave under Section 33 of the Act, the council would have stopped to work, and the ineffective party could attempt to auction the property in debate. In such a situation, the fruitful party can move toward the court and the court can't dismiss in light of the fact that an adequate cure has been allowed under S. 17 of the Act. This judgment likewise fills in as a special case for S. 9(3) of the Act.

Norms relevant to give interval help by Courts. There are no norms recommended to give interval help under S. 9 of the Act. The materialness of arrangements of CPC stays agitated. This was not tended to in the 2015 Amendment Act too. There are two ways of thinking with respect to this. One is the inclusionary approach, and the other is the exclusionary approach. The elite methodology is that the afflictions of CPC can't be set up as it invalidates the point to concede interval under S. 9 of the Act. The other one believes procedures under S.9 to be similar to Order XXXVIII Rule 5 and Order XXXIX of CPC. Request XXXVIII Rule 5 of CPC relates to specific reliefs in nature of award of safety, connection of property or capture of respondents that are like the reliefs under Section 9 (ii) (b) and (c) of the Act. Request XXXIX of CPC accommodates impermanent order likened to the help under Section 9 (ii) (d) and (e) of the Act.

A model for an exclusionary approach is the situation of Tata Capital Financial Services Ltd. v. Solidarity Infraprojects Ltd. and Ors. In this decision the Bombay High Court expressed that the court will extensively remember the Order XXXVIII Rule 5 and Order XXXIX of CPC. Simultaneously, it will likewise have the circumspection to give relief relying on current realities and conditions of the case to get the closures of equity and save holiness of arbitral procedures. A model for an inclusionary approach is the decision of the division seat of Delhi High Court in Anantji Gas Service v. Indian Oil Corporation. For this situation it was held that Section 9 is likened to Order XXXVIII Rule 5 and Order XXXIX of CPC. The prerequisites of these sets of the CPC were held to be vital. The prerequisites are, at first sight case, equilibrium of comfort and unsalvageable misfortune on the off chance that no insurance is advertised.

Principles material to concede interval relief by Arbitral Tribunals. On account of Intertoll ICS (Cecons) O&M Company v. NHAI The court held that the arbitral council would need to find out whether the candidate has presented out a defense according to arrange XXXVIII Rule 5, before giving interval relief. Likewise, on account of Yusuf Khan v. Prajita Developers Pvt. Ltd. furthermore, Ors, it was held that "councils while practicing their power under area 17 and especially Section 17(1)(ii)(b) of the Act, i.e., the standards set down in the CPC for the award of interlocutory cures should outfit a manual for while deciding an application under Section 17 of the Act."

Enforceability of interim relief under S.9 of the Act. Since the request is given by a court, the interim relief will be authorized like some other request of the court. This implies that all regulations pertinent corresponding to orders passed are material on orders under S.9 of the Act also. Enforceability of interval relief under S.17 of the Act. As talked about before, through the 2015 Amendment Act, requests of council were hung comparable to orders of a court. In the new instance of Alka Chandeshwar v. Shamshul Ishrar Khan, the Supreme Court held that rebelliousness of a council's requests added up to scorn and would be offense under the Contempt of Courts Act, 1971. From this one might say that orders under S. 9 and S. 17 of the Act are completely enforceable and are at a similar level.

To finish up from the above composition, one might say that S.9 and S. 17 are not only a procedural matter. It influences the support being given to ADR lately. Prior to the 2015 Amendment, as referenced previously, regardless of the development of council, gatherings would go to the court for a interim measure. Notwithstanding, when the council request was set at standard with a court request, parties went to the court for a interim relief. This decreased the weight of the court, yet additionally diminished the intercession of the legal executive in arbitral procedures. Nonetheless, an opposite assessment to this can be found on account of M.D., Army Welfare Housing Organization v. Sumangal Services Pvt. Ltd. This judgment was conveyed before the 2015 Amendment Act. The court held that an arbitral council isn't an official courtroom and that its requests are not legal orders. It additionally held that the court is to be limited to the four corners of the understanding and pass a request which might be a topic of reference. Nonetheless, it should be noticed that the courts have been outdated and litigative equity has been put to a stop. The requirement for ADR strategies to advance as a subordinate of the legal framework. There is an extreme need to decrease the weight on legal executive and accelerate the method involved with conveying equity. Consequently, to carry S.17 orders at standard with S.9 is a positive development. Notwithstanding the difficulties of the legal executive, feelings against bringing council and court at standard keep on existing, similar to the above Army Welfare Housing judgment. It is to be noticed that Indian regulation doesn't lay a particular capabilities for authorities. Maybe laying off specific capabilities to turn into an authority could lessen such conclusions.

Q5. Explain about the process of appointing the arbitrators under the Act of 199

Answer

The Act of 1996 states that parties can determine the number of arbitrators they wish to appoint however, this should not be an even number. If they are unable to do so, the arbitral tribunal shall consist of a sole arbitrator. The statutory requirement of odd numbers of arbitrators is can be moved away from, which means that if they wish to exercise an option of choosing even number of arbitrators and agree to not to challenge the award thereafter, the award rendered would be a valid and binding. If neither of the parties challenge the composition then any challenge to the composition must be raised by a party before the time period prescribed under the Act, failing which it will not be open to that party to challenge the award after it has been passed by the arbitral tribunal. The Act enables the arbitral tribunal to rule on its own jurisdiction. A challenge to the jurisdiction of the arbitral tribunal cannot be raised, after the submission of the statement of defense although the party might have participated in the appointment of the arbitrator and might have appointed the arbitrator himself. Both parties can choose the arbitrators.

Qualification of Arbitrators

The parties should ideally follow an agreed procedure for appointing the arbitrators. However if that fails and an application is filed in court for appointment, the Chief Justice or the person or institution designated by him, in appointing an arbitrator, shall have due regard to any qualifications required of the arbitrator by the agreement of the parties.[i]

A clause in the agreement, which provides for settling the dispute by arbitration through arbitrators having certain qualifications or in certain agreed manner is ordinarily followed by the courts and not derogated from unless there are strong grounds for doing so. The appointment of an arbitrator can be challenged within 15 days after he learns of the constitution of the arbitral tribunal or after becoming aware of the circumstance that he does not possess the necessary qualification.

It is not open to a party, especially in government contracts, to contend that appointment of only one arbitrator only by one of the parties to the dispute will violate the principle that no man can be a judge in his own cause if that party had voluntarily entered into the contract with knowledge of this fact and had thus accepted the terms and conditions of the contract. The question of its maintainability before the arbitral tribunal stating that the arbitration clause in the contract between the parties is void and unenforceable law cannot be accepted.

Requirements for Filing an Application for the appointment of an arbitrator

The essential pre-conditions to be satisfied before an application for appointment of arbitrator by Court:

(i) There should be an arbitration clause in the contract in terms of section 7;

(ii) The party filing the application should have knowledge of the arbitration agreement;

(iii) There is a dispute between the parties in relation to the contract containing the arbitration agreement.

(iv) A notice invoking an arbitration clause has been issued and received by the other party.

A dispute or difference is a pre-condition of the right to arbitrate and seek an appointment. Mere disagreement on a central issue is sufficient to constitute a dispute, a claim need not necessarily arise. And merely raising a claim cannot satisfy the precondition of the dispute.

Appointment of Arbitrator through Court Assistance

An arbitration agreement as defined under Section 7 of the Act is a condition precedent in order to exercise the power to appoint an arbitrator or an Arbitral Tribunal, according to Section 11 of the Act by the Chief Justice or his designate.

The Supreme Court has identified the duties of the chief justice or his designate.[iii] First they identified and separated the preliminary issues that arise from the application under Section 11 of the Act into three categories, that is:

(i) Issues that the Chief Justice or his designate must decide;

(ii) Issues which the Chief Justice or his designate choose to decide

(iii) Issues that have to be left to the Arbitral Tribunal to decide.

Section 11 of the Act provides for the procedure to appoint an arbitrator or arbitrators with court assistance. The primary objective of seeking court interference under the Act is so that securing the constitution of the arbitral tribunal can happen expeditiously. Parties can agree upon a procedure for appointment of a sole arbitrator or arbitrators as under sub-section (2) of section 11 and can approach the court in the event they don't have a procedure. The court's jurisdiction and the nature of its power as per section 11 has been quoted directly from the judgment

"(i) The power of the Chief Justice of the High Court or the Chief Justice of India under Section 11(6) of the Act is a judicial power.

(ii) The power under Section 11(6) of the Act, in its entirety, could be delegated, by the Chief Justice of that court to another judge of that judge.

(iii) The Chief Justice or the designated Judge will have to decide the preliminary aspects as indicated earlier. These will be his own jurisdiction to entertain the request, the existence of a valid arbitration agreement, the existence or otherwise of a live claim, the existence of the condition for the exercise of his power and on the qualifications of the arbitrator or arbitrators. The Chief Justice or the designated Judge would be entitled to seek the opinion of an institution in the matter of nominating an arbitrator qualified in terms of Section 11(8) of the Act if the need arises but the order appointing the arbitrator could only be that of the Chief Justice or the designated Judge.

(iv) Designation of a District Judge as the authority under Section 11(6) of the Act by the Chief Justice of the High Court is not warranted on the scheme of the Act.

(v) Once the matter reaches the Arbitral Tribunal or the sole arbitrator, the High Court would not interfere with orders passed by the arbitrator or the Arbitral Tribunal during the course of the arbitration proceedings and the parties could approach the Court only in terms of Section 37 of the Act or in terms of Section 34 of the Act.

(vi) Since an order passed by the Chief Justice of the High Court or by the designated Judge of that Court is a judicial order, an appeal will lie against that order only under Article 136 of the Constitution to the Supreme Court.

(vii) There can be no appeal against an order of the Chief Justice of India or a Judge of the Supreme Court designated by him while entertaining an application under Section 11(6) of the Act.

(viii) In a case where the parties have constituted an Arbitral Tribunal without having recourse to Section 11(6) of the Act, the Arbitral Tribunal will have the jurisdiction to decide all matters as contemplated by Section 16 of the Act.

(ix) Orders under Section 11(6) of the Act have been made based on the position adopted in an SC decision, we clarify that appointments of arbitrators or Arbitral Tribunals thus far made, are to be treated as valid, all objections being left to be decided under Section 16 of the Act. As and from this date, the position as adopted in this judgment will govern even pending applications under Section 11(6) of the Act.

(x) Where District Judges had been designated by the Chief Justice of the High Court under Section 11(6) of the Act, the appointment orders thus far made by them will be treated as valid; but applications if any pending before

them as on this date will stand transferred, to be dealt with by the Chief Justice of the High Court concerned or a Judge of that Court designated by the Chief Justice.

For the appointment of an arbitrator under Section 11 of the Arbitration and Conciliation Act, 1996, following are to be kept in mind:

(i) That there is a dispute between the parties to the agreement and it is alive

(ii) That the arbitrator has to be appointed according to the terms and conditions of the agreement and as per the need of the dispute.

Q6. What is Arbitral tribunal? What is the composition of arbitral tribunal? What is the ground for challenging the appointment of the arbitrator? Is there any provision for termination of arbitrator?

Answer

Suit is considered as a dreary cycle. It isn't just tedious yet additionally exorbitant. The motivation behind why private gatherings and establishments have concocted elective methods of question goal. Discretion is one such elective system that is utilized to determine business questions in India. Whenever a business question emerges between two or gatherings, and they choose to determine the debate through intervention, an arbitral council is to be set up. It comprises of at least one authorities that settle and resolve the debate and give an arbitral honor. The Indian Council of Arbitration has given a bunch of rules known as the 'Decides of Arbitration' that are to be complied with the gatherings going through the intervention cycle as well as the authorities. Rule 2 of these guidelines characterizes Arbitral Tribunal as "a referee or judges delegated for deciding a specific debate or distinction" Section 2(d) of the Arbitration and Conciliation Act, 1996 additionally characterizes an arbitral court as a sole authority or board of referees.

Composition of an Arbitration Tribunal

Section III of the Arbitration and Conciliation Act, 1996 (thus alluded to as the 'Act') sets out the arrangements for the Composition of an Arbitral Tribunal. Additionally, Rule 22 of the Rules of Arbitration set somewhere around the Indian Council of Arbitration expresses that when an application for discretion system is gotten, the Council makes essential strides for the constitution of an arbitral court to mediate the questions or contrasts between parties. A few arrangements concerning the organization of an arbitral court are as per the following: Section 10 of the Act makes reference to the quantity of judges that will be a piece of the arbitral council.

As per statement (1) of the Section, the gatherings to the debate are free to commonly conclude the quantity of authorities that will comprise the arbitral council to arbitrate the question. It is, in any case, essential that the quantity of mediators selected will be an odd number and not an even one guarantee that there are no ties. Moreover, Section 10 additionally expresses that assuming the gatherings to the debate can't choose the quantity of authorities, all things considered, just a single mediator will be delegated. Rule 22 of the Rules of Arbitration gives that assuming the worth of the case made under assertion is One Crore or less, a solitary judge can resolve the debate on the off chance that the gatherings consent to it. In situations where the case to the debate surpasses one Crore, the arbitral court will be made out of three mediators with the understanding of the gatherings. In *Narayan Prasad Lohia vs, Nikunj Kumar Lohia,* the Supreme Court observed that if two arbitrators are appointed for an Arbitral Tribunal instead of three, and they give an award through common opinion, there will be no frustration of proceedings.

Procedure for appointment of arbitrators

The procedure and appointment of arbitrators under the arbitral tribunal is specified under Section 11 of the Arbitration and Conciliation Act. It states the following:

1. **Nationality-** The parties to the dispute may, on agreement, appoint an arbitrator belonging to any nationality.
2. **Appointment by Parties-** The procedure to appoint one or more arbitrators can be decided by the parties. If the parties fail to do so, they may individually appoint an arbitrator each, and the two arbitrators, mutually decide the third one.
3. **Appointment by Court-** if the parties do not appoint an arbitrator within 30 days from the receipt of the request, the Supreme Court, the High Court, or any other official designated by the Court may appoint an arbitrator.

In *Golden Chariot Recreations Pvt. Ltd. v Mukesh Panika & Anr.,*the Supreme Court held that a party to the dispute can file an application for the appointment of an arbitrator by the Court only after the expiry of 30 days.

1. **Payment of fees-** the High Court has the authority to frame rules concerning the determination of fees of the arbitral tribunal and the

manner of its payment.

The Rules of Arbitration also provide the manner of the appointment of a sole arbitrator or three arbitrators under Rule 23. According to this rule, on receipt of the application, the Registrar of the Arbitration Committee may ask the parties to the dispute to select an arbitrator from among the Panel of Arbitrators within 30 days. In case of failure, the Registrar himself appoints a sole arbitrator to resolve the dispute between parties. Similarly, the Registrar can also appoint three arbitrators if the parties to the dispute do not arrive at an agreement.

In *Oriental Insurance Company v M/S Narbheram Power and Steel Pvt,* it was held that the arbitration clause under an agreement is to be strictly interpreted. It expresses the intention of the parties to appoint an arbitrator for the settlement of any dispute. This clause cannot be waived off in normal circumstances.

Grounds for challenging the appointment of arbitrators and its procedure

When a person is nominated as an arbitrator, he is required to disclose his past or present connection to either party or parties, whether direct or indirect. Also, he shall disclose if he has a financial, business, professional or any other interest in any of the parties or in the subject matter of the dispute, which may prevent him from adjudicating in an impartial manner. Therefore, as perSection12 of the Act, either party to the dispute may challenge the appointment of an arbitrator on the following grounds:

1. If there is a sufficient doubt that the arbitrator may act in a partial or biased manner.
2. If the nominated arbitrator does not possess the qualifications required by the parties to the dispute.

The appointment of an arbitrator can be challenged in accordance with the procedure mentioned in Section 13 of the Arbitration and Conciliation Act, 1996. Either party can challenge the appointment within 15 days after receiving the knowledge of the constitution of the arbitral tribunal or after the knowledge of circumstances mentioned above. The authority to decide on the challenge is vested in the hands of the arbitral tribunal.

In *Antrix Corp. Ltd. v Devas Multimedia Pvt. Ltd,* the Court held that if any party to the dispute disagrees or is dissatisfied with the composition of the arbitral tribunal, it can approach the Court to challenge the appointment of the arbitrator by way of application.

Not only the appointment of the arbitrator can be challenged but also his mandate can be terminated under Section 14 and 15 of the Act in the following cases:

1. If the arbitrator is unable to carry out his functions in an effective manner or there is an undue delay in the performance of his duties.
2. If the arbitrator himself withdraws from his office or the parties agree to his termination.

Rule 27 of the Rules of Arbitration also states that an arbitrator can be terminated from his mandate on account of his resignation or death, if he is negligent in performing his duties or fails to act in an expeditious manner, and does not declare the arbitral award within a prescribed time.

In ***National Highways Authority of India vs Gammon Engineers and Contract***, the Delhi High Court held that the Arbitral Tribunal is bound by the Arbitration agreement between parties. The Arbitration agreement cannot be rewritten and neither can the tribunal accept an appointment in part.

Substitution of an arbitrator

If an arbitrator is terminated from his mandate, another arbitrator may be appointed as a substitute by following the appointment procedure. In such a case, the arbitral hearings can be repeated at the discretion of the arbitral tribunal. The provisions related to the substitution of an arbitrator are mentioned under Section 15 of the Arbitration and Conciliation Act, 1996.

The Indian Judiciary hosts suggested on numerous occasions that gatherings ought to take up discretion as a debate settlement system to lessen the weight on the courts and for a rapid goal of questions. Hence, a few alterations have been proposed in the Arbitration and Conciliation Act, 1996. Areas 10-15 of this Act and Rules 22-27 of the Rules of Arbitration, sets down arrangements for the creation of an Arbitral Tribunal. This is of most extreme worry in the reception of mediation as a component for debate settlement. The gatherings must pick the right referee or judges that establish the arbitral council so the honor conveyed by the court is fair and just and liberated from any segregation or biasness. It likewise guarantees that the debate is settled in a successful and expedient way.

Q7. Explain about the jurisdiction of the arbitral tribunal.

Answer

Discretion was imagined as a method to stay away from the difficulties looked in the system of common prosecution in courts. In India, it stayed alive right off the bat in the appearance of panchayats, which involved individuals who were approached to decide on issues introduced before them, and their decisions were yielded by the gatherings to the question. The British made the most importantly utilization of the idea of mediation for in the Bengal guidelines of 1772 and 1813 arrangements connected with the discretion of debates were applied to unfaltering property and the Arbitration Act of 1899 was revoked by the Arbitration Act, 1940. These rules chiefly engaged to regulate the technique of assertion in India. In any case, in some span of time, obviously the Arbitration Act of 1940 was not fit to the point of handling the prerequisites of a quickly evolving India. Along these lines, it was subbed by the Arbitration and Conciliation Act in 1996. It depends on the UN Model Law to settle on our regulation concurrence with the law embraced and procured by the United Nations Commission on International Trade Law (UNCITRAL). The Act is of revising and combining in nature and not comprehensive. It has a much-broadened extent of the 1940 Act. It focuses on the homegrown Arbitration and authorization of unfamiliar arbitral awards.

It wouldn't be fitting to say that an arbitral council has legal purview. The court decides its locale to change the necessities of the gatherings. The arbitral understanding mostly decides the ambit of ward of the arbitral council. The central of party-independence announces that when the two gatherings have the solution for resolve their questions on their own then they have the solution for show this option to any outsider, to decide unmistakable that quarrel.

1. Consequently it is exceptionally fundamental to think about a very much drafted arrangement since it brings about giving total solidarity to the council to decide matters connected with the ward. The Arbitration and Conciliation Act, 1996 likewise explicitly specifies the locale to decide express matters in Section 17 of the Act.

   a. Appointment of a gatekeeper for an individual who is of shaky brain or minor age in the middle of the course of intervention

b. Safety/Security/Confinement/temporary order of the topic of the discretion.

There are a few cases wherein the capability of the arbitral court is dependent upon acquiring questions. The important arrangement under the Act (Sec 16). Section 16 of the Arbitration and Conciliation Act gives the accompanying arrangements:

1. The arbitral council might manage or coordinate on its own ward, which additionally joins any complaint with respect to the legitimacy or presence of the intervention arrangement, and for that goal:

a) An assertion condition which is a term of an agreement understanding should be considered as an arrangement free and independent of different terms of the agreement, and

b) A choice of the arbitral council pronouncing the agreement as invalid doesn't require ipso jure the deficiency of the mediation proviso.

2. A supplication which radiates that the arbitral court doesn't have ward will not be made after the guard explanation is submitted; in any case, a party will not be kept from making such a request simply because of his cooperation in the arrangement of, or he named, a judge.

3. A request guaranteeing that the arbitral council is outperforming the extent of its power will be made when the matter affirmed to be risen above the extent of its position is made during the arbitral procedures.

4. In every one of two cases alluded to in sub-section (2) or sub-area (3), The arbitral court might acknowledge a postponed request assuming it closes with an assessment that the deferral is legitimized.

5. The arbitral court will decide the supplication alluded to in sub-section (2) or sub-area (3) and take up with arbitral procedures where the arbitral council takes a choice dismissing the request.

6. A party, whenever displeased by such an arbitral award, may make an application for rescinding such an arbitral award according to Section 34.

Capability of the arbitral court

The Arbitration Act of 1940 needed such arrangements which approved the Arbitral Tribunal to manage on its own locale and it was upon the court to investigate and settle on the purview of the arbitral council. Yet, Section 16 of the Arbitration and Conciliation Act, 1996 awards capacity to the Arbitral Tribunal to look on its own purview. Area 16 (1) of the Act gives that the arbitral council might manage or coordinate on its own locale, which additionally fuses any complaint in regards to the legitimacy or presence of the discretion understanding.

Area 16 of the Arbitration and Conciliation Act fuses the idea of ability skill. It contains two features for example the first mirrors that without help from the courts, the council might settle on its purview and furthermore, it shows hesitance from the courts in concluding this issue before the council has settled on this issue. In any case, questions with respect to the limiting impact of the choices made by the arbitral councils should be examined and would these choices be able to be tested in courts?

In Union of India versus M/s. East Coast Boat Builders and Engineers Ltd., the Hon'ble Delhi High Court saw that it was evident from the plan of the demonstration that the assembly didn't allow request against the request under Section 16(5) where the arbitral council concludes rejects a supplication that it has no purview. Evidently, the goal is that the arbitral council will continue with the arbitral procedures and make an award right away and without obstruction at any stage in the arbitral cycle because of administrative job of the court.

On account of Nav Sansad Vihar Coop. Bunch Housing Society Ltd. (Regd.) versus Smash Sharma and Associates the Hon'ble Delhi High Court held that assuming the Arbitral Tribunal dismisses a request under Section 16(5) of the Arbitration and Conciliation Act, the arbitral cycle will occur and the award will be proclaimed and in the mean time, the oppressed party will stand by till the award is reported and there is no cure against such request.

However, assurance made by the council to concede the supplication that it doesn't have locale or that it is outperforming its ambit of power is appealable and offense under Section 37(2) of the Arbitration and Conciliation Act. On account of Pharmaceutical Products of India Ltd. versus Goodbye Finance Ltd., the Hon'ble Bombay High Court believed that in situations where the Arbitral Tribunal dismisses the supplication connected with its locale, Section16(5) of the Arbitration and Conciliation Act plainly enables the Tribunal to continue with the arbitral procedures and pronounce an arbitral award. Section 16(5) awards system to challenge an arbitral award. It expresses that just as per Section 34, such an award can be tested. though, assuming the Arbitral Tribunal decides to acknowledge the supplication that it doesn't have locale, then, at that point, such choice can be pursued under Section 37(2) of the Arbitration and Conciliation Act.

Accordingly, obviously when the Arbitral Tribunal chooses to dismiss a request that it doesn't have the locale then the request made connected with its purview can't be pursued however when the Arbitral Tribunal acknowledges the supplication that it doesn't have ward then such a request can be pursued under Section 37(2) of the Arbitration and Conciliation Act.

Jurisdiction of the arbitral council when contract it is void to contain an intervention statement

There might be situations where the mediation understanding isn't settled on as a different arrangement. All things considered, it is implanted, as a condition, in the arrangement between the gatherings and such agreement or the understanding between the gatherings is articulated void or illegal. The inquiry which emerges is that what befalls the arrangement in such cases and would the assertion condition in such cases be able to become void?

On account of Jawaharlal Burman versus Association of India, the Hon'ble Supreme Court held that it is hypothetically conceivable that the agreement might end and the discretion agreement may not and comparatively it is likewise hypothetically conceivable that the agreement might be substantial while the intervention understanding might be void and in that sense, there is a distinction between the agreement and its important for mediation arrangement yet experiencing the same thing, a test to the actual agreement incorporates a test to the assertion understanding. On the off chance that there is a closed agreement the assertion statement is additionally substantial and in the event that there is certainly not a finished up agreement the intervention condition is likewise invalid. The Court likewise recognized that there could be a larger part of cases in which the assertion arrangement exists as a piece of the fundamental agreement itself, and testing the legitimacy or even presence of one would mean a test to the legitimacy or presence of others.

On account of Waverly Jute Mills Co. Ltd. Versus Raymon and Co. (India) Ltd., The Hon'ble Supreme Court thought that talk to the authenticity of an agreement could be the topic of an arrangement of intervention comparatively as a discussion relating to a case made under the agreement. Be that as it may, such an understanding would be usable and successful just when it is unmistakable from and autonomous of the agreement which is questioned as illicit.

On account of Jaikishan Dass Mull versus Luchhiminarain Kanoria and Co., the Hon'ble Apex Court of India thought that there can't be any questions that in the event that an agreement is void and unlawful, the assertion condition should likewise die alongside the actual agreement. As Viscount Simon, L.C. likewise brought up in Heyman versus Darwins Ltd.

that assuming one party to the agreement battles that it is void stomach muscle initio, and for this view, the actual proviso is void and along these lines the intervention statement can't work. The discretion proviso, which is a fundamental substance of the agreement, can't stand assuming that the actual agreement is announced to be illicit.

Be that as it may, the position has changed after the order of The Arbitration and Conciliation Act in 1996. Also, Section 16 (1) of this Act pronounces that the intervention provision regardless of whether embedded in an agreement, will be considered as a free from the excess of the agreement and an assurance made by the Arbitral Tribunal in regards to the deficiency of the agreement will not need ipso jure nullification of the discretion condition.

On account of Olympus Superstructures versus Meena Vijay Khaitan, the Apex Court expressed that it will be seen that the arbitral council is currently engaged under sub-section (1) of Section 16 of the Act to look and reexamine on its own ward which additionally remembers choosing for any protest connected with the legitimacy or even presence of the intervention understanding and for such reason, the discretion statement which is a piece of the agreement and any choice by the arbitral council connected with the shortcoming of the agreement will not need ipso jure influence the legitimacy of the assertion provision. It is obvious from proviso (b) of Section 16(1) which gives that a choice by the arbitral court connected with negation of the principle contract will not need ipso jure nullification of the assertion statement.Deficiency of skill of arbitral court to manage on its own

Section 11(6) of the Act expresses that a party might engage the assign of Chief Justice or the Chief Justice himself to make essential strides when agreed by the gatherings under an arrangement technique, one of them doesn't go about as important under the system, or the two arbiters miss the mark to adhere to an understanding as pondered of them under the method, or an individual or establishment misses the mark to execute a capacity invested to him under the strategy.

What's more, Section 11(7) pronounces that a goal which is taken by the Chief equity or the individual assigned by him under Section 11(4), Section 11(5) or Section 11(6) will be conclusive. It shows that a restriction of the court to reexamine its own purview when the Chief Justice has thought of and chosen it.

On account of Konkan Railway Corporation Ltd. versus Rani Construction Pvt. Ltd. the judgment held that for a situation when the main equity or any individual assigned by him might have named the mediator through the thirty days had not lapsed then the Arbitral Tribunal could never have been comprised appropriately and accordingly be without locale. The wronged party, all things considered, could require the Arbitral Tribunal to lead on its purview and Section 16 gives arrangement to this and pronounces that the Arbitral Tribunal might look on its locale.

On account of Sundaram Finance Ltd. versus NEPC India Ltd., the Hon'ble Supreme Court held that a request expressed under Section 11 of the Act is a regulatory request. It implies that no allure could exist under Article 136(1) of the Constitution. This case shows reluctance with respect to the Court to influence the opportunity appreciated by the assertion cycle and by pronouncing that the elements of the Chief Justice are authoritative, the Court had basically prohibited the Chief Justice from settling questions like the legitimacy or presence of the discretion arrangement.

Section 16 of the demonstration can't be pronounced to enable the Arbitral court to fail to acknowledge the choice which is given by the legal power or the Chief equity before the reference to it was made. The position to choose doesn't allow the Arbitral council to overlook the certainty conceded to a request passed before to its entering upon the reference by the exceptionally resolution which makes it. Accordingly, assuming the Chief Justice or an individual assigned by him has investigated the legitimacy or presence of the discretion arrangement and on its ward then the Arbitral Tribunal can't reevaluate the subject of its purview. It would in such a case be illegal from investigating the question of its purview.

Enforcement of the arbitral awards

The method for execution of pronouncements in India is represented through the Code of Civil Procedure, 1908 while that of arbitral awards is administered through the Arbitration and Conciliation Act, 1996 ("Act") as well as the CPC.

On account of Sundaram Finance versus Abdul Samad and Anr, a two-Judge Bench of the Hon'ble Apex Court of India had cleared the questions connected with the ward for the authorization of the arbitral award. The Supreme Court eliminated the uncertainty by referencing that an arbitral award under the Arbitration and Conciliation Act, 1996 can be released in any court of skillful ward and that getting an exchange request from any court. It was positively a milestone judgment that drawn out the ambit and force of the arbitral council.

The appeal of arbitral awardsn

There can be no allure of arbitral awards against the purview connected with the benefits of the arbitral award. The Hon'ble Supreme Court has seen that a referee ought to be considered as an adjudicator which is named by the gatherings and an award passed by him ought not be softly impeded. In one judgment, the Supreme Court pronounced that the thought of the award being good can't be chosen exclusively on the reason of the drive of any individual. Nonetheless, this doesn't imply that the arbitral award is outright and it doesn't keep from scrutinizing the consequence of intervention.

There are sure cures which are made by the law to guarantee legitimate and proficient direct of procedures. The revoked Arbitration and Conciliation act 1940 Act gave three cures against an assertion grant which are alteration, abatement and saving which has been additionally revised by the Arbitration and Conciliation Act, 1996 and the cures are partitioned into two sections. Also, the solution for correction of blunders has been given over the Tribunal and to the gatherings to choose.

The solution for saving is corrected and the award after the mediation cycle will be gotten once again to the court for evacuation of imperfections. Section 34 gives a grounds to save the arbitral award which incorporates an invalid understanding, the confusion, shortcoming with respect to one of the gatherings, inadequacy in the subject of the assertion cycle and the arbitral award, restricting the public arrangement, an error in the arrangement of the referees and so on

The Act of 1996 determines that an arbitral award can't be upset by the court just on account of re-enthusiasm for proof or a mistaken utilization of the law. On account of Brijendra Nath versus Mayank, the Hon'ble Supreme court announced that if during the pendency of the application testing the legitimacy of the arbitral award, the gatherings have followed up on it, then, at that point, it would prompt estoppel against going after the award.

Hence, the discretion began as a technique to keep away from the difficulties of common prosecution. English Government spread it in India. The Arbitration Act, 1940 centered to organize the system of mediation in India. Later this act was corrected by the Arbitration and Conciliation Act of 1996. An arbitral court doesn't have legal locale. The court decides its own locale to change the requirements of the gatherings. The arbitral understanding fundamentally decides the ambit of locale of the arbitral council. There can be no allure of arbitral awards against the locale connected with the benefits of the arbitral award. Section 11(7) announces that a goal which is taken by the Chief equity or the individual assigned by him under Section 11(4), Section 11(5) or Section 11(6) will be conclusive. It shows that a constraint of the court to reevaluate its own locale when the Chief Justice has thought of and chosen it.

8. Discuss the rules regarding arbitration proceedings as mandated under the Act of 1996.

Answer

The standards in intervention procedures are obligatory as the standards of regular equity are to be continued in substance to guarantee that things are in a state of harmony and that a fair outcome has been given completely. Section 18-27 of the Arbitration and Conciliation Act, 1996 arrangements with the guidelines in regards to the assertion procedures. It is depicted beneath:

Section 18 to 27 of the Arbitration and Conciliation Act, 1996 referenced the standard in regards to the lead of arbitral procedures. Prior to concentrating on these standards, it will be appropriate to express that the Arbitral procedures require all parties to be treated with equity and they ought to be offered sensible chance to communicate their perspective. (Section 18) This implies that the Arbitral will undoubtedly act autonomously and without predisposition. They are expected to be not at fault for unfortunate behavior. They are additionally not expected to act during the shortfall of the parties. As a matter of fact this is the fundamental equation of free and fair procedures.

The primary guidelines for the lead of arbitral procedures are adhering to:

Idea of Rules: According to section 19 of the Act, the parties are given the option to decide the strategy for the lead of arbitral procedures. Parties can choose the standard through an understanding. Arbitral Tribunal is expected to adhere to these guidelines. In the event that the parties don't decide the standard of the methodology then arbitral council will lead the procedures by such strategies which it thinks for.The arrangements of code od common system, 1908amd Indian Evidence Act 1872 doesn't matter over the strategy of direct of arbitral procedures. The judge will undoubtedly keep the Technical guidelines of the code of common methodology and proof Act. It is required only to follow the guideline of normal equity. (Delhi Nagar Nigam Versus Jagannath Ashok Kumar, A.I.R. 1987 S.C. 2316).

In the case of P.R. shah Shares and Stock Broker Private Limited Versus Messer B.H.H. Securities Private Limited (A.I.R. 2012 S.C. 1866), it has been propounded by the supreme court that the Arbitral should not use his own knowledge regarding the dispute during the proceedings. He may use his technical knowledge in respect of any trade- special.

The power of the Arbitral Tribunal including the power to determine the admissibility, relevance, materiality and weight of any evidence. The court cannot interfere in such matters. (Food Corporation of India versus N.B.O. shipping co. 1996 park Arbitration law Report 276 Mumbai; Shankarlal Mazumder Versus State of West Bengal, A.I.R. 1994 Kolkata 55).

Place of Arbitration: The primary right to decide the spot of Arbitration hosts been given to the parties. The parties can decide the spot of Arbitration. On the off chance that the parties neglect to do as such, the Arbitral Tribunal while considering the accompanying, the point can decide the spot of assertion as indicated by the accommodation of the parties.. Arbitral Tribunal can organize its meeting at any of the places for the following purposes

a.   for the consultation with the members
b.   for hearing the witnesses, experts and parties
c.   for inspection of the document goods or other properties etc. (Section 20).

Whatever place is decided by the Arbitral Tribunal the notice of it is required to be given to the parties.(Uttar Pradesh Forest Corporation Versus Vishwanath Goswami, A.I.R. 1995 Allahabad 351)

In the case of the International Airport Authority of India Versus Mohinder Singh (A.I.R. 1996 Mumbai 167), it was stated that Arbitration can change the place of Arbitration for the convenience of parties.

Commencement of Arbitral proceedings: Section 21 of the Act gives the arrangements to the date of initiation of procedures. As indicated by it If the Arbitration Agreement doesn't make reference to the date of initiation of the arbitral procedures, the Arbitral procedures in regard of that question start on the date on which a solicitation for that debate to be alluded to Arbitrator is gotten by the respondent. In the case of Wazir Chandra Versus Union of India (A.I.R. 1973 Guwahati 100), it has been held that the Arbitral should satisfy himself before starting arbitral proceedings that whether the reference is within the stipulated time or not.

Language: The language to be embraced by the Arbitral Tribunal for Arbitral procedures will be what is concurred by the parties. Without even a trace of such arrangement, language will be chosen by the Arbitral Tribunal (segment 22).Language ought to be such which the Arbitrator can comprehend. In the case of E. Rathore and Sons Versus Carlo Bedrida and Co. [(1961)1 Lyod's Report 220], it has been stated that if any documents are in a foreign language which the Arbitrator does not understand, then such documents are required to be translated in the language in which the Arbitrator understand.

Statement of Claim or Defence: Section 23 of the Act lays down that:

a. Within the period of time agreed upon by the parties or determined by the Arbitral Tribunal, the claimant shall state the fact supporting his claim, the points at issue and the relief or remedy sought, and the respondent shall state his defence in respect of these particular.
b. The parties may submit with their statements all documents they consider to be relevant or may add a reference to the document or other evidence they will submit.
c. Unless otherwise agreed by the parties, either party may amend or supplement his claim or defence during the course of the arbitral proceedings, unless the Arbitral Tribunal considered inappropriate to allow the amendment or supplement having regard to the delay in making it.

Here, it is important that the grant of permission to amend depends upon the discretion of the tribunal. Such permission could be granted in any case. (Union State Neyari Versus Lanza Veneer (1917) 2 K.B. 558)

Hearing: Section 24 of the Act provided for the hearing and written proceedings. As indicated by it, the tribunal will choose whether to hold an oral hearing for the introduction of proof or for oral contention, or whether the procedures will be directed based on records and other materials. The Arbitral Tribunal will hold a meeting, at a suitable phase of the procedures, on a solicitation by a party except if the parties have concurred that no oral hearing will be held. The parties will be given adequate notification ahead of time of any consultation and of any gathering of the Arbitral Tribunal with the end goal of investigation of archives merchandise or other property.

All assertion, archives or other data provided to, or application made to the Arbitral Tribunal by one party will be imparted to the next party, and any master report or evidentiary record on which the Arbitral Tribunal might depend in settling on its choice will be conveyed to the parties.

In the case of Damodar Prasad Gupta Versus Saxena and Company (A.I.R. 1959 Punjab 476), it has been held that the parties have complete right to produce their arguments before Arbitral Tribunal. They also have the right to have communication of place and time of the hearing. Of an award is made ignoring this right of parties, it shall be liable to be set- aside.

In the case of R.S. Avtar Singh and Co. Versus N.P.C.C Ltd. (A.I.R.1993 Delhi 230), it was stated that a party should be allowed sufficient opportunity to present their defence and explain a particular fact. Ignoring it would be misconduct.

In the case of Union of India versus Sohan Singh Sethi [(1996)1 Arbitration law Report 504 Delhi] it has been stated to the extent that not hearing the evidence when they were promised of the hearing was a good ground to set – aside from the Award.

The default of a party: It has been specified under segment 25 that where the inquirer neglects to impart his assertion of guarantee, the Arbitral Tribunal will end the proceedings.Where the respondent neglects to convey his assertion of guard the Arbitral Tribunal will proceed with the procedures without regarding that disappointment in itself as a confirmation of the charges by the petitioner.

Where a party neglects to show up at an oral hearing or to deliver narrative proof, the Arbitral Tribunal might proceed with the procedures and make the arbitral honor on the proof before it. In the case of Anil Jain Versus Madhuna Appliances Pvt Ltd. [(1997) 2 Arbitration law Report 32-5 Delhi] it has been held that if the parties do not remain present even after the notice, the Arbitrator shall have the right to have ex- part proceedings against them.

In the case of Messer Senbow Engineering Ltd Versus State of Bihar (A.I.R. 2004 Patna 33), it has been held by the Patna High court that the Arbitral Tribunal under section 25(a) has the right to terminate the proceedings and can re-cancel such an order on having sufficient grounds.

Appointment of Experts: Section 26 provides the right to Arbitral Tribunal to appoint Experts for correct disposition of the dispute. It shall be the duty of parties to given the expert any relevant information or to produce, or to provide access to, any relevant documents goods or other property for his inspection.

Court assistance in taking evidence: As per section 27 of the act, the parties of arbitral proceedings or arbitral tribunal may take help of court for assistance in giving or taking evidence. For this purpose, the Arbitral Tribunal, or a party with the approval of the Arbitral Tribunal may apply to the court for assistance in taking evidence. The following points are to mention in the application a) Name and address of parties and Arbitrator, b) General nature of the claim and wanted relief, c) Evidence to be obtained.

Q8. Discuss exhaustively on making of arbitral awards and termination of proceedings.

Answer

Secs. 28-33 of the Arbitration and Conciliation Act, 1996 deals with the making of arbitral awards and termination of proceedings. The provisions regarding the same are discussed below as follows:

Making of arbitral award and end of procedures is totally tended to with in CHAPTER VI of the Arbitration and Conciliation Act, 1996. From sections 28 to 33 everything revolves around "making of arbitral award and end of procedures". This examination paper will not exclusively legitimize the significant exposed arrangements anyway will likewise lay explicit accentuation on Section 32. This section manages the "End of procedures".

The job of a arbitrator is to determine disputes that the parties have in consent to submit to assertion. The choices of the arbitrator require an archive subject to specific conventions, and alluded to as the arbitral award. The substance and type of an arbitral award, and furthermore the carefulness appreciated by judges in making an award can basically change as per the procedural regulation material to the arbitral strategy, the powers introduced by the parties upon the arbitrator under the relevant discretion understanding, and furthermore the particular kind of assertion utilized.

Arbitral Award under Arbitration and Conciliation Act, 1996

As per the definition given under Section 2(c) obviously the 1996 Act doesn't give a substantial meaning of Arbitral awards. It exclusively insists that arbitral awards incorporate between time awards as well. Be that as it may, a definitive call given by the arbitral council [as per Section 2(d)] is the arbitral award.

In like manner, an arbitral award could be characterized as the limiting and ultimate conclusion made by an arbitral council or a sole arbitrator, that purposes, entirely or to some degree, the question submitted to his/its locale.

The award can give a spread of solutions for the parties relying upon the issue of the dispute. This include:

a. Injunctive Remedies: Once a court orders that a party ought to make a move or stop an activity, it's called a directive. An authority might offer similar award in a question any place one party needs such help.
b. Money: Several award can conclude that one party should pay the contrary party in view of the agreement or dispute controlling the award.
c. Interim Relief: Typically, the question between the parties can have a few hidden feelings and interests that are driving the parties. Though the judge won't have as much opportunity as a middle person to help the parties come to a sensible arrangement, a arbitrator could host one get-together issue a conciliatory sentiment or give a positive business reference.
d. Incentives: A judge could add motivations for specific ways of behaving to urge the parties to suits the award.

The Calcutta High Court portrayed an arbitral award because of the consensual equity of the parties. Inside the instance of Bhajahari v. Bihari arbitral award was illustrated as the last assurance of the case or issue, by a judge willingly. In Harinarayan Bajaj v. Sharedeal Finance, it was held that according to definition under Section 2 an arbitral award incorporates a break award. Nonetheless, a between time award to be an award needed to decide a case with irrevocability. When the not set in stone, the Tribunal couldn't arbitrate all the more consequently guarantee and become functus officio. Besides, the procedural orders passed all through the arbitral procedure is basically rejected from the idea of award. In Paradise Hotel v. Air terminal Authority of India Ltd, the implementation of an award is finished just when it has been carried out under CPC inside a similar way as though small a pronouncement of court. In Pandit Munsi Ram and partners v. Association of India, it was deciphered that since an arbitral award is considered an announcement as under Section 35 of the 1996 Act, the court held that an arbitral award is a request which decides the privileges of parties required by at last deciding the real case or issue inside the course of arbitral procedures.

Types of Arbitral Award under Arbitration and Conciliation Act, 1996
There are two kinds of awards:

a) Domestic awards this kind of award is represented under Part I of the Act: according to Section 2(7), Domestic awards, are out and out managed to a limited extent one till Section 43 of the Arbitration and mollification act though Sections 44 to 60 arrangement with various types of unfamiliar arbitral awards. The arbitral award is worth exclusively to the degree of the parties' capacity to authorize the terms they stomach muscle initio recommended. Section 36 sets down arrangements for the quick requirement of the domestic awards. Under this very section, it is clarified that a domestic award is enforceable inside the very way as that of an announcement passed by a court. In domestic discretions, on the off chance that the resources of the parties are practically in very much the same purview, the authorization of domestic award bountiful more straightforward. Also, upholding an arbitral award than judgment by a court is more straightforward.

b) Foreign awards this type is hence represented under Part II: Part II of Chapter 1 arrangements with the New York Convention awards. In this Section 48 arrangements with the refusal of authorization of the unfamiliar award. Part 2 Section 57 arrangements with the arrangements in regards to the authorization of Geneva Convention awards.

In *Serajuddin v. Michael Golodetz*, the Calcutta High Court laid down the essential conditions of a 'foreign arbitration' where the award is further called a foreign arbitral award, the main points of this case were:

1. Arbitration should have been held in foreign a foreign country
2. By a foreign arbitrator
3. Arbitration by applying foreign laws
4. One of the parties consists of foreign national.

Provisions of Arbitration and Conciliation Act, 1996 dealing with Arbitral Award

Section 28 of the Arbitration and Conciliation Act, 1996

An Arbitrator ought to choose the dispute in equity and with sincere intentions. Notwithstanding, there's a condition point of reference, considering that each parties explicitly approve a arbitrator to settle then exclusively he will choose the dispute between them.

Domestic interventions ought to keep Indian assertion regulation. Notwithstanding, for worldwide assertions arrangements basically situated in India, the arbitral council ought to keep the regulations the parties have consented to apply in their consent to resolve questions. The chose regulation as concurred inside the understanding ought to be interpreted except if explicitly concurred in any case.

It ought to likewise be remembered that while applying the law of a novel general set of laws, the meaningful laws of India ought not be in struggle with them. Inside the shortfall of any such arrangement or any sign of what might be the pertinent regulations once a dispute emerges, the arbitral council will apply regulations that are material and applicable to the question.

Moreover, the arbitral court ought to apply arrangements exclusively predictable with the conditions of the agreement between parties. Nonetheless, the court ought to moreover consider the uses and furthermore the current exchange rehearses that are pertinent to the agreement.

An Arbitrator ought to choose the question in equity and sincerely. Notwithstanding, there's a condition point of reference, considering that each parties explicitly approve an authority to settle then exclusively he will choose the question between them.

Domestic mediations ought to keep Indian intervention regulation. In any case, for worldwide assertions arrangements basically situated in India, the arbitral court ought to keep the regulations the parties have consented to apply in their consent to resolve disputes. The chose regulation as concurred inside the understanding ought to be interpreted except if explicitly concurred in any case.

It ought to likewise be remembered that while applying the law of a one of a kind overall set of laws, the meaningful laws of India ought not be in struggle with them. Inside the shortfall of any such arrangement or any sign of what might be the material regulations once a question emerges, the arbitral council will apply regulations that are appropriate and pertinent to the dispute.

Moreover, the arbitral council ought to apply arrangements exclusively reliable with the provisions of the agreement between parties. Notwithstanding, the court ought to moreover consider the utilizations and furthermore the current exchange rehearses that are applicable to the agreement.

Section 29 of the Arbitration and Conciliation Act, 1996

The choice of the Arbitral Tribunal will be in the greater part. The arbitral award is the definitive phase of the arbitral procedures. The decision made by most of the individuals from the council will be pronounced as an award.

Section 30 of the Arbitration and Conciliation Act, 1996

Section 30 allows the consolation settlement among the parties by the arbitral court. On the off chance that the parties with progress adjust to a settlement, the equivalent can be joined inside the type of an award. Such settlements are recorded on the grounds that the Arbitral award based on concurred conditions. Such genial arbitral awards ought to be make as per Section 31. It makes the similar end result and status as that of an arbitral award passed by a free council to substance a question.

Section 31 of the Arbitration and Conciliation Act, 1996

As per Section 31 Arbitral awards will be in marked and composing by every one of the individuals from the council. The explanation applied behind the award ought to be express obviously. Nonetheless, on the off chance that the parties have concurred for settlement, not a great explanation behind an arbitral award based on concurred conditions, should be exhibited. The date of announcement of an Award and furthermore the spot any place it's made will be referenced. Spot of the award is furthermore called as the seat of intervention. A copy of the award will be given to each party. Arbitral Tribunals can likewise pass a between time award.

In the case of *Sukanya Holdings Pvt. Ltd. v. Jayesh H. Pandya*, non-signatories to an arbitration agreement can even participate in arbitration proceedings as long as the necessary and proper parties to the agreement are present. This is often to both Indian seated International Commercial Arbitration and domestic arbitration.

Termination of Arbitral Proceedings under Arbitration and Conciliation Act, 1996

Section 32 of the Arbitrational and Conciliation Act, 1996 is totally coherent with Article 32 of UNCITRAL Model Law. According to Section 32(1) of the Act termination of Arbitral proceedings takes place once the final award declared by the arbitral tribunal. The other three grounds of termination of arbitral proceedings are given under Sub-section 2 of Section 32.

To terminate the arbitration proceedings arbitral tribunal shall issue an order:

a. The parties themselves agree to terminate the proceedings.
b. If the arbitral tribunal finds that the continuation of the proceedings is either unnecessary or impossible for any other reason.
c. the plaintiff withdraws their claim. It can also be terminated if the respondent objects to the arbitral award. Looking at which the arbitral tribunal come to a conclusion that it has a legitimate interest in obtaining a final settlement.

In the last, The mandate of the arbitral tribunal will terminate with the termination of the procedure itself. Sub-section (3) of this section lays down that the above provisions are subject to Section 34(4) and section 33.

In the case of *Sai Babu v. M/S Clariya Steels Private Limited*, in 2019 the Supreme Court held that once the sole arbitrator terminates the arbitration proceedings under Section 32(2)(c) of Arbitration and Conciliation Act, 1996 ("Arbitration Act"), the same cannot be subsequently recalled. In order to reach a conclusion in the case of Sai Babu v. M/S Clariya Steels Private Limited the Apex Court chalked out a difference between the termination of Arbitral proceedings under Section 32 and Section 25 of the Arbitration and Conciliation Act.

The case of *SREI Infrastructure Finance Ltd v. Tuff Drilling Private Ltd.* where it stated that "On the termination of proceedings under Section 32 sub-section (1) and (2), Section 32 sub-section(3) additional contemplates termination of proceedings by Arbitral Tribunal on any other grounds or due to the fact that carrying out the arbitral proceedings is needless. The conditions laid down under section 32 is missing in Section 25. However, if the claimant shows decent cause as to why he desires the arbitral proceedings then it may be recommenced. The Apex court conjointly noted that section 32(3) provides for the termination of the mandate of the Arbitrator once a termination order is passed under section 32.

Subsequently, the end of procedures strategy and making an arbitral award set down is really direct and basic. The Supreme Court has some of the time think of recommended alterations and vital translations. It's intriguing to take note of that the end of arbitral procedures is different under Section 32 and Section 25. The convincingness of award denotes the end of procedures under Arbitration and Conciliation Act under Section 32 alongside three different grounds. Not several radical judgments are passed with regard to the above subject however Sai Babu v. M/S Clariya Steels Private Limited holds good law.

Q9. Discuss the grounds on which an arbitral award can be challenged.

Answer

Arbitration is a genuine procedure, which occurs outside the courts, and simultaneously brings about a last and legally confining choice like a court judgment. Intervention is a versatile system for question objectives, which can give a fast, modest, secret, sensible and last answer for a debate. It incorporates the affirmation of the debate by somewhere around one free outcasts rather than by a court. The untouchables, called judges, are named by or to serve the social occasions in debate. The arbitration is driven according to the provisions of the gatherings assertion understanding, which is by and large found in the game plans of a business contract between the gatherings.

All things considered, this understanding is oftentimes made before the debate arises and is fused as a condition in their business contract. In denoting a concurrence with an assertion stipulation, the gatherings are agreeing that their question will not be heard by a court, yet by a private individual or a leading group of a few private people groups. Assuming the gatherings have agreed to arbitration, they will all things considered need to go to intervention, rather than the court. As the courts will normally decline to hear their case by remaining it to propel the reluctant party to regard their consent to parley.

Grounds for setting aside an arbitration award

Domestic Arbitral award: An award supported in assertion which happens in India would be a "domestic award". extra, an award made in a worldwide business discretion held in a non-show country is likewise estimated to be a "domestic award".

The difficulties to the arbitral awards are managed part VII under the head 'Plan of action against arbitral award'. This part has just a single segment for example Segment 34. The part manages saving the arbitral award. This segment depends on Article 34 of the UNCITRAL Model with not many deviations. The appropriateness of segment 34 is restricted to the awards made in India or domestic awards. The authority subsequent to making the award records something very similar in the court. The party wanting to have the award saved should create an application to the court under which an award can be tested on the grounds referenced in area 34 of the Act. The Court can act just when such an application is made by a party. There is no unique structure endorsed to make the application. The segment records the justification for it are comprehensive to save which.The remedy under this section is available only in case of domestic arbitration. Thus, an application filed under this section for setting aside an award made in connection with a contract relating to international commercial arbitration will have no applicability.

An award can be set aside only in the three contingencies:

a. The composition of arbitral tribunal was not in accordance with the agreement;
b. The arbitral procedure was not in accordance with the agreement between the parties;
c. In the absence of such an agreement, the composition of the arbitral tribunal or arbitration procedure was not in accordance with Part I of the Act.

An award will be totally void if:

a. The arbitrator was not truly designated or needed vital capabilities.
b. The parties never settled on any limiting arbitration arrangement.
c. The matters in question fell external the extent of the understanding.
d. The entire of the help allowed lay external the powers of the authority.

It is obvious from an uncovered perusing of segment 34 that the award can be saved provided that any of the five grounds as contained in segment 34(2)(a) or any of the two grounds as contained in segment 34(2)(b) of the Act exist. The extent of obstruction with the award is extremely restricted and is confined to the grounds referenced in this part. The utilization of the word 'just' is genuinely critical and it prohibits a place of assault against an arbitral award other than those examined under area 34(2) (a) and (b) expressed in this segment and no more. Any ground other than the one recorded in the segment might be summoned. Subsequently it is important to analyze these grounds intently.

Notwithstanding area 34, there are a few extra justification for saving awards. Segment 13 of the 1996 Act accommodates a test to an authority on the ground of absence of freedom or absence of capability or nonpartisanship. An application for the test in the principal occurrence is to be made before the arbitral court itself. Segment 13(5) of the 1996 Act gives that where the council overrules continues and challenge with the discretion, the party requesting the authority might make an application for saving the arbitral award under segment 34 of the Act. Thusly, the way to deal with a court is simply at the post-grant stage.

Foreign Arbitral award: Part II of the Act of 1996 arrangements with the Enforcement of Certain Foreign Awards. It has two sections. Part I, area 44 to 50, manages New York Convention grants; and part II, segment 53 to 60, manages Geneva Convention grants. The arrangements of Part II of the Act of 1996 give impact to both the New York Convention and the Geneva Convention.

As per both UNCITRAL Model Law and New York Convention, any response against an arbitral award including the chance of a cancellation is passed on to the public courts of the country wherein the discretion has its seat. The Act of 1996 accommodates saving procedures against an arbitral award under Section 34, which falls inside Part I of the Act; though the implementation cycle would be according to Part II of the Act.

To be considered as an unfamiliar award (for the motivations behind the Act), the equivalent should satisfy two prerequisites;

a) It should manage contrasts emerging out of a lawful relationship (regardless of whether legally binding) considered as business under the regulations in force in India.

b) The country where the award has been given should be a show country. A show nation is a part nation of the New York Convention and informed by the Government of India in the Official Gazette It is by and large acknowledged that a global arbitration grant is conclusive and restricting.

The legislature does not believe in leaving the aggrieved party through the arbitral award without any remedy and has ensured to incorporate a provision that can allow appeals to higher courts in certain cases on valid grounds mentioned thereof, making it in consonance to the principles of natural justice.

In case one of the parties fear or have substance to believe that the arbitrator is prejudiced, biased or does have the jurisdiction on the matter, an application before the arbitrator itself is filed under Section 13 of the Act. In case the arbitrator sets it aside and continues the proceedings, leading the party to find themselves at a loss through the award pronounced; then the arbitral award can be challenged in the Hugh Court under Section 34, stating this prejudice as the preliminary ground. Hence, the legislature seems to have served a dual purpose- a) limiting the interference of the judiciary in arbitration and b) providing the required remedy to the aggrieved parties.

Section 34 provides that an arbitral award may be set aside by a court on certain grounds specified therein, which are as follows:

a. the enforcement of the award would be contrary to Indian public policy.
b. the parties to the agreement are under some incapacity;
c. the subject matter of dispute cannot be settled by arbitration under Indian law; or
d. the agreement is void;
e. the award contains decisions on matters beyond the scope of the arbitration agreement;
f. the award has been set aside or suspended by a competent authority of the country in which it was made;
g. the composition of the arbitral authority or the arbitral procedure was not in accordance with the arbitration agreement

A court judgment can be pursued for genuine and lawful audit. In any case, an arbitral award regularly must be tested in view of procedural inconsistencies, absence of purview, and absence of arbitrability or infringement of public strategy. The English Arbitration Act of 1996 licenses bid on a mark of English regulation in the event that all gatherings concur or the court awards pass on to pursue. The court's ability to allow leave, nonetheless, is limited and requires the court to establish that goal of the inquiry will significantly influence the freedoms of at least one gatherings and that the inquiry was one the council was posed to choose. It further requires the court to verify that the council's choice was clearly off-base or "the inquiry is one of overall population significance and the choice of the court is basically open to genuine uncertainty."

There are a few necessities for an unfamiliar arbitral award to be enforceable under the Act of 1996.

a. **Commercial exchange:** The award should be given in a show country to determine business debates emerging out of a lawful relationship.
b. **Written understanding:** The Geneva Convention and the New York Convention give that an unfamiliar arbitral arrangement should be made recorded as a hard copy, in spite of the fact that it needs not to be phrased officially or be as per a specific organization.

c. **The arrangement should be legitimate:** The unfamiliar award should be substantial and ought to emerge from an enforceable business understanding.

d. **The grant should be unambiguous:** To give impact to an award, it should be clear, unambiguous and fit for goal under Indian regulation.

In **Sanjeev Kumar Jain v. Raghubir Saran Charitable Trust, (2012) 1 SCC 455,** the supreme court of India has dealt the important arrangements under the Code of Civil Procedure, 1908 for the award of compensatory and correctional expenses for the successful party. The Supreme Court in this landmark judgment has recommended a climb in the quantum of expenses on people enjoying negligible and vexatious cases, which are stopping up the equity conveyance framework in the nation.

The Supreme Court, following its earlier decision, in appeal in **Bhatia International vs Bulk Trading S. A. & Anr 2002,** Trading held that even though there was no provision in Part-II of the Act providing for the challenge to a foreign award, a petition to set aside the same would lie under Sec. 34- Part I of the Act. The Court held that Indian Law necessarily would need to be followed to execute the award. The Court held that a challenge to a foreign award in India would have to meet the expanded scope of Public Policy as laid down in Saw Pipes Case i.e. to meet a challenge on merits contending that the award is 'patently illegal'.

In **Oil & Natural Gas Corp. v. Saw Pipes Ltd., in 2003** The Supreme Court prescribed four facets while elaborating on the meaning of the expression 'public policy of India' in context of Section 34 and only the test of "patent illegality" is inapplicable to a challenge to enforcement of foreign awards under Section 48 of the Act.62 Thus, the principles enunciated in this case, being part of "fundamental policy of Indian law" are applicable to domestic and foreign awards alike.

Along these lines, the Parliament has requested the Arbitration and Conciliation Act in order to give convenient fix by assertion and to achieve this objective, area 5 of the Act puts a total bar on the intercession of the courts in issues where there exists a discretion articulation. The law of assertion in India is, especially at its crossing point. As things stand today, assertion is prepared to affect uncommon changes to the way question goal is directed. It conveys with it the earnestness and unalterable quality of the lawful system and couples it with the procedural adaptabilities of forward thinking debate objectives strategies. There is, notwithstanding, a comparatively squeezing need to essentially upgrade the arbitral systems in India. In any case, specifically, we feel that there is a need to affect a change in acknowledgment. As our nation moves towards extending bellicosity, elective strategies for debate objectives might just give the best approach to settling the issues of overburdened caseloads, long pendency of cases and an extremely unending example of value being conceded.

Q10. Write in short about the finality of the arbitral award and its enforcement.

Answer

Finality of Arbitral Award under Section 35 of the Act of 1996

It is given under section 35 of the Arbitration and Conciliation Act, 1996 that the award after a discretion continuing will be restricting on the gatherings to the procedures.

At the point when an arbitral award is made it is in entirety concerning every one of the aspects and suggests that no more advances can be additionally taken by the arbitral council. The award hosts a limiting impact on the gatherings.

An award by an arbitral court is final when:

a) The Period that is given to make an allure testing the award in the court terminates;

b) And in conditions when a party has recorded an application in the court testing the award and the equivalent gets dismissed.

Implementation of arbitral award: Section 36 of the Arbitration and Conciliation Act, 1996 after the 2015 Amendment Act, gives that when the time span that is accommodated making an application in the court for saving an arbitral award has terminated the award of the arbitral council will have an impact of a pronouncement of a court and will be upheld similarly. (According to the arrangements of Code of Civil Procedure of 1908).

Assuming that a party difficulties the award of an arbitral council (under section 34 of the Arbitration Act) by recording an application for the equivalent in the court, since he has applied wouldn't save the arbitral award. The award will be saved just when the court orders so.

The court might put a stay on the arbitral award assuming it is fulfilled that the award is contrary to the standards of equity. The court will record its justification for doing as such.

The impact of 2015 change is that before the alteration of 2015 to section 36, assuming an award is tested in the court, it would suggest a programmed stay on the arbitral award. Be that as it may, presently the position has been changed and the arrangement of the programmed stay on the award by applying has been scratched out. This was significant as the party abused by the award would utilize the recording of an application testing the award as an unreasonable instrument to put a stay on the arbitral award.

Presently, for putting a stay on an arbitral award there will be a particular request from the court.

Enforceability of section 36

Section 36 of the Arbitration Act is pertinent just in issues inside India. The arrangements connecting with Foreign Awards and its implementation are administered by Section 48 of the Arbitration Act.

Q10. Discuss about the New York Convention and Geneva Convention as far as the enforcement of arbitral award is concerned that is covered under the provisions of Arbitration and Conciliation Act, 1996.

Answer

With the expansion of international trade in recent years, the business world has been increasingly reluctant to litigate in courts of law for differences arising from international commercial transactions. Ability to communicate with and commute to distant places with the utmost speed enables a merchant in a few minutes or hours, to conclude a contract abroad which a generation ago would have taken weeks or months. However, when it becomes necessary to resort to the machinery of justice to settle a dispute connected with that contract, to enforce a judgment in another country is still a complicated, time-consuming and expensive operation. It is not surprising, therefore, that businessmen have been turning with increasing frequency to arbitration as a quicker and simpler means of settling international commercial disputes. There has been a noticeable movement in favour of arbitration. Arbitration facilities and institutions have increased over time. The favourable trend towards arbitration has been reflected in legislative enactments, international treaties and other measures by which arbitration has gradually acquired a more solid legal standing.

India forms a vital cog of the wheel of the global economy. The ever-increasing level of globalization has led to raise international business disputes too. In this context, the enforcement of foreign judgment and foreign Arbitral Awards becomes significant. A foreign judgment may be enforced in India either by proceedings in execution or by a suit upon it. An arbitral award is a determination on the merits by an arbitration tribunal in arbitration, and is analogous to a judgment in a court of law. Arbitration is particularly popular as a means of dispute resolution in the commercial sphere. One of the reasons for doing so is that in international trade, it is often easier to enforce an arbitration award in a foreign country than it is to enforce a judgment of the court. The enforcement of foreign arbitration awards in India is governed by the Arbitration and Conciliation Act, 1996 through New York Convention and Geneva Convention and a non- conventional award will be enforceable in India under the common law grounds of justice, equity and good conscience

Prior to January 1996, the law of enforcement of arbitration awards in India was spread between three enactments. Enforcement of domestic awards was dealt with under Arbitration Act, 1940. Enforcement of foreign awards was divided between two statutes- a 1937 Act to give effect to the Geneva Conventionawards and a 1961 Actto give effect to the New York Convention awards.

GENEVA CONVENTION

On the international level, there are numerous bilateral treaties including provisions for the enforcement of arbitral awards. As to multilateral treaties, the most significant developments since the First World War have been the Geneva Protocol on Arbitration Clauses of 1923, the Geneva Convention on the Execution of Foreign Arbitral Awards of 1927, and the United Nations Convention on the Recognition and Enforcement of Foreign Arbitral Awards of 1958. The application of both treaties is limited to persons who are subject to the jurisdiction of different contracting states. Under the Protocol, an arbitration agreement relating to existing or future differences is recognized as valid, that is, irrevocable. The agreement may relate to any matter capable of settlement by arbitration, but the contracting states may limit their obligations to commercial contracts. If a suit is brought despite the arbitration agreement, courts are required to refer the parties to the arbitrators, except where the agreement or the arbitration cannot proceed or has become inoperative. The Convention is supplementary to the Protocol in that it applies to awards made pursuant to arbitration agreements covered by the Protocol. Only states parties to the Protocol may become parties to the Convention. Each contracting state is required to recognize as binding and to enforce, in accordance with the procedure of the forum, awards rendered in the territory of another contracting state, on the following conditions:

a) The award was rendered pursuant to arbitration agreement valid under the law applicable to the agreement;

b) The object of the award is capable of settlement by arbitration under the law of the country of the forum;

c) The award was rendered by the arbitral tribunal provided in the arbitration agreement or constituted as agreed by the parties and in conformity with the law governing the arbitration procedure;

d) The award has become final and no proceedings are pending for the purpose of contesting the validity of the award. An award still subject to opposition or appeal or the equivalent is not regarded as final;

e) The recognition or enforcement of the award would not be contrary to public policy or the "principle of the law" of the forum.

Even where these conditions have been met, recognition and enforcement of the award must still be refused if the court finds that:

a) The award has been annulled in the country where it was rendered; or

b) The party against whom the award has been invoked did not have sufficient notice, or being under a legal incapacity, was not properly represented; or

c) The award deals with a dispute not included under the terms of the agreement, or the award goes beyond the scope of the agreement. Furthermore, a court may refuse enforcement or give the losing party reasonable time to seek annulment if that party proves that under the law of the country where the arbitration took place, there is a ground (other than those specified in the Convention) to contest the validity of the award in a court of law.

The Geneva treaties have been criticized for the following legal and practical reasons:

a) There is some ambiguity in the expression "subject to the jurisdiction of different Contracting States" which defines the scope of application of the treaties. It is not clear whether it means subject to the sovereignty of a state in the sense of nationality, or subject to the jurisdiction of the courts of a state by reason of residence, domicile, or other criteria.

b) It has also been observed that a plaintiff seeking enforcement in one country would find it particularly difficult to prove that the arbitral tribunal was constituted in conformity with the law of another country and that the award has become final in that country.

c) Finally, the possibility of contesting the validity of an award on grounds other than those listed in the Convention has been regarded as making it too easy for a recalcitrant defendant to avoid the enforcement of an award by resorting to obstructionist tactics.

This state of affairs prompted the International Chamber of Commerce, which had originally taken the initiative leading to the Geneva Convention, to submit to the United Nations Economic and Social Council a proposal for a new convention on the enforcement of international arbitral awards. In the opinion of the ICC, the main defect of the Geneva Convention was the condition that to be enforced, an arbitral award must be "strictly in accordance with the rules of procedure laid down in the law of the country where arbitration took place." In order to meet the requirements of international trade, the ICC advocated the idea of an 'international award, i.e., an award completely independent of national laws, and suggested that arbitral awards based on the will of the parties should be automatically enforceable. The ICC draft sought to attain this purpose mainly by widening the scope of application and providing that, as a condition for enforcement, the composition of the arbitral authority and the arbitral procedure must be in accordance with the agreement of the parties. Only in the absence of such agreement, they should conform to the law of the country where arbitration took place. The other conditions for enforcement in the ICC draft did not differ greatly from those of the Geneva Convention, except for the omission of the requirement of finality of awards, regarded by the ICC as encouraging dilatory measures

NEW YORK CONVENTION

The United Nations Convention on the Recognition and Enforcement of Foreign Arbitral Awards, i.e. the New York Convention, aims to facilitate the recognition and enforcement of arbitral awards generally between private parties. It succeeds the 1927 Geneva Convention on the Execution of Foreign Arbitral Awards and the 1923 Geneva Protocol on Arbitration Clauses (which also provided for reciprocal recognition and enforcement abroad of certain arbitration agreements and awards, but had serious shortcomings). It is described as the most successful treaty in private international law and is adhered to by more than 140 nations.

The New York Convention was established as a result of dissatisfaction with the Geneva Protocol on Arbitration Clauses of 1923 and the Geneva Convention on the Execution of Foreign Arbitral Awards of 1927. These conventions suffered from certain shortcomings. For example, they excluded from their application awards rendered in a state not a party to the Geneva Convention, and required orders enforcing the award in the country where the award was rendered as well as the enforcing country. They also placed the burden of proof on the party seeking to enforce the award, while at the same time making it all too easy for a recalcitrant defendant to avoid enforcement by resorting to delaying tactics. The New York Convention sought to remedy these problems.

The initiative to replace the Geneva treaties came from the International Chamber of Commerce (ICC), which issued a preliminary draft convention in 1953. The ICC's initiative was taken over by the United Nations Economic and Social Council, which produced an amended draft convention in 1955. That draft was discussed during a conference at the United Nations Headquarters in May-June 1958, which led to the establishment of the New York Convention.

There are two basic actions contemplated by the New York Convention:

a) The recognition and enforcement of foreign arbitral awards, i.e., arbitral awards made in the territory of another State: This field of application is defined in Article I. The general obligation for the Contracting States to recognize such awards as binding and to enforce them in accordance with their rules of procedure is laid down in Article III. A party seeking enforcement of a foreign award needs to supply to the court- the arbitral award and the arbitration agreement. The party against whom enforcement is sought can object to the enforcement by submitting proof of one of the grounds for refusal of enforcement which are listed in Article V, paragraph 1. The court may on its own motion refuse enforcement for reasons of public policy as provided in Article V, paragraph 2. If the award is subject to an action for setting aside in the country in which, or under the law of which, it is made ("the country of origin"), the foreign court before which enforcement of the award is sought may adjourn its decision on enforcement. Finally, if a party seeking enforcement prefers to base its request for enforcement on the court's domestic law on enforcement of foreign awards or bilateral or other multilateral treaties in force in the country where it seeks enforcement, it is allowed to do so by virtue of the so called more-favourable-right provision.

b) The referral by a court to arbitration: Article II, paragraph 3, provides that the court of a Contracting State, when seized of a matter in respect of which the parties have made an arbitration agreement, must, at the request of one of the parties, refer them to arbitration. The influence of the New York Convention on the development of international commercial arbitration has been phenomenal. The New York Convention solidified two essential pillars of the legal framework by providing for the obligatory referral by a national court to arbitration in the event of a valid arbitration agreement and for the enforcement of the arbitral award. The New York Convention is probably the main reason why arbitration is the preferred method for the resolution of international business disputes.

The New York Convention applies to all arbitral awards rendered pursuant to a written arbitration agreement in a country other than the State of enforcement. The New York Convention also applies to arbitral awards not considered as domestic awards by the enforcing state. The term 'arbitral award' is not defined, but includes awards made by ad hoc tribunals as well as permanent arbitral tribunals. The nationality of the parties is irrelevant for purposes of the convention. Under Article I(3), the contracting States can choose to limit the application of the convention to arbitral awards rendered in another contracting state or to awards relating to commercial disputes.

In order to obtain recognition and enforcement of an arbitral award under the New York Convention, a party only has to supply the enforcing court with a certified copy of the arbitral award and the arbitration agreement. If an arbitral award is encompassed by the New York Convention, contracting states must recognize the award as binding and enforce it in accordance with local rules of procedure. They may not impose more onerous conditions, higher fees, or charges on the recognition or enforcement of the award than prevail with respect to domestic arbitral awards. If a party objects to enforcement, then it is under a burden of proving that the award should not be enforced. The objecting party must argue under Article V(1) which provides a list of grounds for refusing enforcement:

1. Invalidity of the arbitration agreement;
2. Violation of due process;
3. Excess by arbitrator of his authority;
4. Irregularity of arbitral tribunal,
5. Suspension of the award.

Additionally, the court can refuse to enforce the award if its subject matter is incapable of settlement by arbitration under the enforcing country's laws or if recognition or enforcement of the award would violate the enforcing country's public policy. As the Geneva Convention became virtually otiose (by reason of Art VII of the New York Convention), enforcement of foreign awards, for all practical purposes, came under the

1961 Act and domestic awards came under the 1940 Act. The enforcement regime between these two statutes was, however, quite distinct. The 1961 Act confined challenge to an arbitral award only on the limited grounds permitted under the New York Convention.

FOREIGN ARBITRAL AWARDS IN INDIA: THE NEW REGIME

In January 1996, India enacted a new Arbitration Act. This Act repealed all the three previous statutes (the 1937 Act, the 1961 Act and the 1940 Act). The new Act has two significant parts. Part I provides for any arbitration conducted in India and enforcement of awards there under. Part II provides for enforcement of foreign awards. Any arbitration conducted in India or enforcement of award there under (whether domestic or international) is governed by Part I, while enforcement of any foreign award to which the New York Convention or the Geneva Convention applies, is governed by Part II of the Act. In other words, it is the provisions of Part II of the Act that give effect to the New York Convention and the Geneva Convention.

In order to be considered as a foreign award for the purposes of the Act, the same must fulfill two requirements. First it must deal with differences arising out of a legal relationship (whether contractual or not) considered as commercial under the laws in force in India. The expression 'commercial relationship' has been very widely interpretated by the Indian courts.

"The term 'commercial' should be given a wide interpretation so as to cover matters arising from all relationships of a commercial nature, whether contractual or not. The second requirement is more significant and that is that the country where the award has been issued must be a country notified by the Indian government to be a country to which the New York Convention applies."

The second requirement is more significant. The country where the award has been issued must be a country notified by the Indian Government to be a country to which the New York Convention applies.Only a few countries have been notified so far and only awards rendered therein are recognized as foreign awards and enforceable as such in India.

An interesting issue came up before the Supreme Court as to what would happen in a case where a country has been notified but subsequently, it divides or disintegrates into separate political entities. This came up for consideration in the case of *Transocean Shipping Agency Pvt. Ltd* v. *Black Sea Shipping*.Here the venue of arbitration was Ukraine which was then a part of the USSR — a country recognized and notified by the Government of

India as one to which the New York Convention would apply. However, by the time disputes arose between the parties the USSR had disintegrated and the dispute came to be arbitrated in Ukraine (which was not notified). The question arose whether an award rendered in Ukraine would be enforceable in India notwithstanding the fact that it was not a notified country. Both the High Court of Bombay (where the matter came up initially) and the Supreme Court of India in appeal, held that the creation of a new political entity would not make any difference to the enforceability of the award rendered in a territory which was initially a part of a notified territory. On this basis the court recognized and upheld the award.

This decision is of considerable significance as it expands the lists of countries notified by the Government by bringing in a host of new political entities and giving them recognition in their new avatar also At another level the judgment demonstrates the willingness of Indian courts to overcome technicalities and lean in favour of enforcement